DODGING ENERGY VAMPIRES

Also by
CHRISTIANE NORTHRUP, M.D.

BOOKS

A Daily Dose of Women's Wisdom*

Making Life Easy*

Goddesses Never Age*

Mother-Daughter Wisdom

The Secret Pleasures of Menopause*

The Wisdom of Menopause

The Wisdom of Menopause Journal*

Women's Bodies, Women's Wisdom

The Secret Pleasures of Menopause Playbook*

Beautiful Girl*

AUDIO/VIDEO PROGRAMS

Goddesses Never Age*

Creating Health

The Empowering Women Gift Collection
with Louise L. Hay, Susan Jeffers, Ph.D.,
and Caroline Myss, Ph.D.*

Making Life Easy*

Menopause and Beyond*

Mother-Daughter Wisdom

The Power of Joy*

The Secret Pleasures of Menopause*

Women's Bodies, Women's Wisdom

Inside-Out Wellness
with Dr. Wayne W. Dyer*

MISCELLANEOUS

Women's Bodies, Women's Wisdom
Oracle Cards*

*Available from Hay House
Please visit:

Hay House USA: www.hayhouse.com®
Hay House Australia: www.hayhouse.com.au
Hay House UK: www.hayhouse.co.uk
Hay House India: www.hayhouse.co.in

DODGING ENERGY VAMPIRES

AN EMPATH'S GUIDE TO EVADING RELATIONSHIPS THAT DRAIN YOU AND RESTORING YOUR HEALTH AND POWER

CHRISTIANE NORTHRUP, M.D.

HAY HOUSE, INC.
Carlsbad, California • New York City
London • Sydney • Johannesburg
Vancouver • New Delhi

Published and distributed in the United States by: Hay House, Inc.: www
.hayhouse.com® • *Published and distributed in Australia by:* Hay House
Australia Pty. Ltd.: www.hayhouse.com.au • *Published and distributed
in the United Kingdom by:* Hay House UK, Ltd.: www.hayhouse.co.uk •
Distributed in Canada by: Raincoast Books: www.raincoast.com • *Published in India by:* Hay House Publishers India: www.hayhouse.co.in

Cover design: Nita Ybarra • *Interior design:* Pamela Homan
Indexer: Laura Ogar

Cataloging-in-Publication Data is on file at the Library of Congress

Hardcover ISBN: 978-1-4019-5477-2

10 9 8 7 6 5 4 3 2 1
1st edition, April 2018

Printed in the United States of America

To Lightworkers everywhere.
Our time has finally come.

CONTENTS

INTRODUCTION

I've spent a lifetime working in the field of health and healing—first as a conventionally trained ob/gyn physician and surgeon and then later as a global teacher who reminds women about everything that can go right with their bodies. And, even more important, how to make this their reality.

During my decades on the front lines of women's health, I have seen countless women suffer from seemingly inexplicable health conditions. These women eat well. They exercise. They take care of themselves. They manage families, jobs, homes. On paper, everything looks great, but each time I dig deeper into their lives, I find that there is another person at the root of their problems—a person who seems to be literally sucking the life blood from them. I refer to these people as energy vampires.

Most of the women (and also men) afflicted by energy vampires are compassionate, loving, and deeply concerned about the well-being of the people around them. They interact with the energy of other people to a degree that puts them well past being merely compassionate. They don't simply feel an observational sadness when they see someone suffer; they feel the same suffering, as if they are having a firsthand experience of the pain they are witnessing. These women fall into a category of people known as empaths. My guess is that if you're reading this, you recognize yourself a bit in this description.

Until quite recently, energy vampires have been largely unrecognized and undiagnosed by society in general and the medical and legal systems in particular. That's why so few people understand what a problem they are.

I didn't actually realize the degree to which they affected the lives of my patients until I began researching them because of what was happening in my own life. As an empath, I mistakenly believed that everyone shared the same empathy and compassion that I have. I assumed that no matter how much harm someone was causing to their families or colleagues that deep down, in their heart of hearts, they were good people who meant well. They were simply acting out of their unexpressed pain and denial. It never occurred to me that there are people who are actually predators—who prey on the agreeableness, trust, goodwill, openheartedness, and resourcefulness of others. I couldn't imagine that there were people who are nearly devoid of empathy, compassion, caring, and the willingness or even capacity to change. But this is exactly what energy vampires are. They are chameleons who can be master manipulators, getting what they want from others without giving anything in return.

Unsuspecting empaths often open their hearts, their bank accounts, and their bodies in order to help these vampires heal their so-called wounds, which actually don't exist. This is not because the empath is a fool. It results, instead, from the perfect storm of the empath's desire to be a healing force in the world, combined with the predatory skills of the vampire—and, very often, the unhealed wounds of the empath, who often doesn't feel worthy of the best life has to offer.

The truth of this was brought into stark focus for me by a series of romantic relationships and with several close friends and some business colleagues. These relationships were sapping me. I felt like I was going crazy. Losing myself. I was always blaming myself and feeling like I needed to improve something. What was I doing wrong? As it turns out, the only thing I was doing wrong was over-giving to people I thought I could heal without including my own needs and well-being in the mix. I had no idea that many people in my life were energy vampires.

This is actually the case for so many people who form relationships with energy vampires. We don't even know that we're dealing with one of these masters of Darkness until we become physically ill, lose our friends, our jobs, our incomes, our fertile years, and eventually even our self-esteem and dignity.

The thing about energy vampires is that they target the people who are most likely to put up with their tactics—and those people are empaths, because we have extremely high levels of compassion and empathy. The energy vampires know just how to use this to their own benefit—and to the detriment of the empath.

But there is hope. The mental health profession in particular and society in general is finally getting up to speed on how these energy suckers work—and how predictable they are. They are identifying personality traits and manipulation tactics. They are figuring out how to recognize vampires and opening up new pathways to leave these relationships.

That's why I've written this book. I wanted to bring together some of the best research that's been done about this topic and combine it with the experiences from my own life and the lives of my global community members to provide clear advice for exiting and healing from unhealthy relationships. In Part I of the book, I lay the foundation for understanding the players in vampire-empath relationships and how and why they interact the way they do—and what effect that can have on your life. And then in Part II, I guide you through straightforward processes to turn the focus back onto yourself so you can heal and avoid energy vampires in the future. I do want to note, however, that healing from vampire abuse is a relatively individual endeavor. Obviously, there are some things that everyone must do, but your healing process will look different from everyone else's. Think of this book not as a road map to healing but as a smorgasbord of techniques. Some of them will make sense in your life, others won't. Choose the ones that work for you. I promise that if you follow the advice in this book, you'll be able to ditch the Darkness and create radiant health, brilliant relationships, and a joyful life.

As an empath, you have special gifts that bring light to the world. Your compassion and empathy are healing salves for the people around you and the planet itself. You were not put on earth to be the energy source of a vampire. You are here to bring your light to the world.

PART I

UNDERSTANDING THE DYNAMICS

Chapter 1

A HIGHLY SENSITIVE SOUL

If you've found this book, it's likely you have a sneaking suspicion that one of your relationships isn't 100 percent healthy. It could be a relationship with a parent, a spouse, a co-worker, a sibling, a child, or anyone else you spend a good amount of time with. You may love and respect this person, but every time you are with them, you come away feeling a little crazy. You may also feel drained, depleted, and tired—like the energy has literally been sucked out of you. If this sounds familiar, it's likely that you are in relationship with someone who is commonly known as an energy vampire. People who fall into this personality category feed off the energy of the people around them.

The other thing that is likely is that—just like the energy vampire—you also have a personality type. Tell me if any of this sounds familiar. You go somewhere and find yourself suddenly feeling sad—or angry—for no apparent reason. Perhaps you know immediately after settling in at a movie theater or concert that you have to sit elsewhere. Or perhaps someone who seems happy leaves you feeling extraordinarily sad. Maybe you feel drawn to the healing arts and the study of things like astrology and energy medicine, but feel like you can't tell anyone about it because they'll think you're crazy. Perhaps you're not so sure that you are worthy enough to deserve love and attention without earning them through acts of service.

If you can relate to anything like this—or if you've simply been told that you're "too sensitive"—it's likely that you are part of a special group of individuals called empaths, or highly sensitive people. There's been a lot of talk lately—and even some best-selling books—about empaths. In fact, in her endorsement of Judith Orloff's book *The Empath's Survival Guide*, world-renowned medical intuitive Caroline Myss refers to empaths as "the new normal."

One thing to keep in mind is that not all empaths are the same. Some are simply highly sensitive to the environment around them and to the feelings of others. Others are what I call the "old-soul empaths." These people have lived hundreds—maybe thousands—of lifetimes and are born with heightened levels of traits such as resourcefulness, self-direction, optimism, and loyalty. Regardless of the type, however, all empaths are highly sensitive to energy.

Empaths interact with the energy around them in a way that is different from even a very compassionate person. While the compassionate person may feel bad after seeing someone suffer, an empath actually picks up the true energy of the individual. They can sense the deep, often unseen, pain of the people near them because the energy of that pain shifts their very being. The energy of the people around them, not merely the emotions, affect the well-being and energy of empaths. Empaths take on whatever energy is around them, whether good or bad. And they can't not feel it.

As an empath myself, I have experienced absorbing negative energy firsthand, and it is extremely strange when it happens. When I was at a board meeting of the American Holistic Medical Association years ago, there was another doctor who seemed nice but was also quite opinionated and difficult to pin down. As soon as the meeting was over, I was overcome with nausea. I actually had to run to the bathroom to vomit. I was like a sponge—soaking up her negativity. It had seeped into every cell of my body, and throwing up was the only way my body knew how to cleanse itself. Years later, I came to understand that she was an energy vampire.

Because of our natural proclivity to take on others' energy and mistake it for our own, I often use the word *porous* to describe empaths. We often don't know where we end and another person begins. I have a friend who had to stop going to 12-step meetings because she found herself picking up on all the emotional pain of those in the room, and she couldn't stop crying. Don't get me wrong. Twelve-step meetings can be life-changing as not only healing places but also sources of community. But if you are an empath, you may find the unprocessed—and unfelt—emotions of others a bit too overwhelming. Without the proper self-knowledge and tools to protect yourself, the harm of taking in these powerful emotions may be greater than the good that comes from working the steps and being with others who have lived through similar things.

Sometimes the pain of being an empath can be very disturbing. I have another extraordinarily empathic friend whose ability to take on the energy of others actually results in physical illness. On a regular basis, her body takes on the illnesses of family members, but here's the part that some people find hard to believe. She gets the full-blown symptoms of their illnesses *before* they do. Four months before her father was diagnosed with lung cancer, she had lung symptoms that were so severe that the doctors thought she had lung cancer. And months before another family member got a brain tumor, she developed headaches and all the symptoms of a brain tumor. All of these symptoms went away the moment the family member got their diagnosis and she no longer had to "carry" their energy. While this isn't common, it does illustrate just how powerful the energy of others can be in the life of an empath.

THE EMPATH'S DAY-TO-DAY

So what does the life of an empath look like? The short answer to this is "hiding." Empaths often take extreme measures to contort their true identities into something less painful. They become very good at blending in and figuring out how to be loved and accepted not for who they really are but instead for how they can serve others. For example, if an empathic homosexual child is born into a very conservative family, that child will very quickly know how to suppress his true self in service to his family's belief system. Or if an empathic, creative, energetic child is born into a family that values logic and study, the child will soon become subdued and work to prove her worth through family-approved pursuits.

Empathic children don't do this consciously. It's a survival mechanism. Because they are so attuned to other people's energy, they suffer when others suffer, so they work hard not to make anyone suffer.

This desire to not rock the boat is something that empaths carry with them throughout their lives. They say yes when they want to say no, simply because they don't want to experience the negative energy of the people around them. They take on extra work so other people won't get overwhelmed. They listen to the woes of their friends and family members, offering up suggestions and help. They sacrifice their own well-being for the good of the people around them. Because it's all about the energy.

As children, some empaths don't just display this sensitivity; they also have the ability to see into other dimensions. They see angels, or spirit guides, or other imaginary friends who are not imaginary at all. Often young empaths will make statements about a person's true nature—a nature that isn't obvious to the people around them. For example, a highly sensitive child might very well say something about wanting to avoid Uncle Pete (who later turns out to be a pedophile)—or that Aunt Sally is going to die (right before she does).

But, just as in the examples above, these empathic children soon learn that seeing "things unseen" is deemed bad or wrong. They may be criticized, silenced, or even punished for speaking up about the truth that they feel so acutely.

Intuitive John Holland tells a story of being able to see dead pets around their former owners. As a child, he'd go up to people and talk to them about their dog that died—because he clearly saw that dog right there. This upset and confused people, and he told me that he learned very early on to avoid speaking about what he saw. He learned that his perception was not acceptable to most people and to the beliefs of our society.

The traits that make empaths "different" create a great deal of emotional pain for them. They are wounded—shamed, abandoned, or betrayed—by their families and societies. They are told that they're "weird" or "crazy" or "bad," which in turn leads to anxiety and self-doubt. The thing is, empaths are just like everyone else in their need for acceptance, love, and support, so they start the hiding I mentioned. They bend themselves into pretzels in order to fit in and be loved. Or at the very least, avoid punishment or mocking. Many empaths learn how to override their sensitivity and shut down their intuitive knowing. Some even turn to drugs and alcohol to numb their perceptions.

The other form of hiding that empaths do is more physical. Highly sensitive people tend to avoid crowds. (Think rock concerts or New Year's Eve in Times Square. Or a casino in Las Vegas.) The energy is simply too intense.

They also avoid scary or violent movies or television shows because they are too painful to watch. I spent the first half of the movie *Saving Private Ryan* in the ladies' room because I couldn't handle the depiction of the landing at Omaha Beach during World War II. It was way too difficult to experience on the big screen (or even a little screen for that matter). And when the fight scene in *Cinderella Man* started, I left the theater and stayed outside in the hall—peeking my head in now and then to see when it was over. I am also unable to stomach shows like the popular *Orange Is the New Black*, *Game of Thrones*, and *Breaking Bad*. They are just too violent.

The same thing was true for me as a teenager. My friends often wanted to go to horror movies, and they always invited me. So once, I tried to go—and I walked out during the opening credits because the music was just too spooky.

Another form of physical "hiding" some empaths do is a bit strange—we often hide from technology. Not because we don't like it or understand it, but rather because highly sensitive empaths have different energy systems that can cause technology to malfunction.

I have an empath friend who kept buying watch after watch. No matter what type it was or how expensive it was, the result was always the same: The watch stopped on his wrist. And it remained dead no matter what batteries he put in it. His energy literally drained the batteries. This is because empaths not only absorb energy, they also emit high-frequency energy.

The empath's technology curse goes beyond watches to cell phones, computers, and pretty much any other form of technology. If they can use a cell phone and computer at all—and some can't—they find that their energy messes up the electrical system, making the computer or cell phone do strange things. For example, I was talking to my sister on my cell phone on the very day I wrote this section, and twice, even though I didn't touch the phone, it started dialing another number—in the middle of our conversation. I have other empathic friends with whom our calls get dropped repeatedly. Even on landlines. It's become kind of a joke. When we call each other back after the phone goes dead, we kid (or maybe not) that the dark forces must be listening in and don't want us to talk!

These technological difficulties definitely don't happen for all empaths but if you've experienced odd, inexplicable frustrations with your electronics, perhaps this is why.

One of the most extreme cases I've seen of energy interacting with nearby material is empaths who literally turn off lightbulbs with their energy. This happens most often when the empathic individual is feeling strong energy—like anger—and that energy is messing up three-dimensional electronic devices, not to mention flying in the face of what we believe about "reality."

Many empathic people are also extremely sensitive to smells. They can't tolerate scents that are made from artificial chemical ingredients, though naturally occurring scents like lilacs are just fine. They can also pick up the scent of something being "off" with food—or even with other people—long before most others notice it. You know the phrase, "I can smell when something is off"? They really can.

INNATE STRENGTH AND GOODNESS

With everything I've told you about being highly sensitive, I suspect you're wondering about how to cure yourself from this horrible affliction, right? Well stop right there. Being empathic may have disadvantages, but if you know how to embrace who you really are, the pros outnumber the cons a million to one.

The differences between being an empath and an average person go well beyond taking on the energy of those around you.

Empaths are often extraordinarily skilled healers because they naturally feel into the emotions of others—and may even experience these in their own bodies. Their energy field quite literally goes into the body of another and feels what's going on. Plus they are resourceful enough to be genuinely helpful in nearly every situation. As a result, they often create an atmosphere in which people feel safe, seen, heard, and held. They may also have the ability to take away painful feelings in others—in part by transmuting those feelings within themselves and then sending out cleaned-up energy like a human air purifier. Often after an interaction with an empath, a person will walk away feeling better without knowing why.

When I was five years old, I had a baby sister—named Bonnie Laurie—who died. At the moment of her passing, my life shifted from being a carefree child to being someone who attempted to heal my mother's grief. My empathic nature led me to take on her pain. This may have helped her get through the sorrow—I'll never know, really. But I do know that, on a larger scale, it led to my career in health care that has helped millions of women around the globe. When I moved into this role as my mother's caretaker, I found a place where I could excel and be accepted.

As a child, I didn't realize that this was my form of hiding. I actually didn't realize it until just recently when I was working with a bodyworker who does a type of bodywork that brings up buried memories and emotions that are stored deep in the fascia of your body. As we were working together, he asked me if I had a sister who died. I immediately thought of my sister Cindy, who had been killed in a car accident right after college, but upon further questioning, I realized that the pain I needed to heal actually stemmed from Bonnie Laurie's death. During our work together, I "saw" my five-year-old self in a cowgirl outfit, galloping across the stage in a school play. When I relayed my vision to the therapist, he said, "That's when you abandoned yourself." I wanted to fall to the floor weeping, because I realized just how true that was. I hadn't known that I was taking on my mother's grief. All I knew was that I could make her feel better.

Even though so many healers are highly sensitive empaths, many in conventional medicine don't want to admit this because this ability is seen as so unscientific. One of my colleagues had healing ability in his hands, but he never told anyone about it because he couldn't explain it scientifically. All he knew is that his patients often got better when he touched them. He felt heat in his hands when this was happening. Even though we were close, I didn't find this out until his sister mentioned it at his funeral and shared what a dilemma it had been for him.

In addition to these healing abilities, highly sensitive people also tend to experience the joys of the world more fully. The sun shines pure ecstasy into their souls. Music reaches deep within, calling forth tears or ecstatic wonder. Movement speaks to them at a cellular level. I can't tell you how much pure happiness I experience while I dance the tango or play my harp—something I've been doing more as I embrace my sensitivity and recover from my need to rescue others.

Because of their ability to sense energy around them, empaths are often drawn to animals and nature because of their calming and innocent energy. This attraction can be a powerful motivation to do good in the natural world— working to protect the least among us, be it the earth itself or the animal inhabitants on it.

Despite what our society believes and rewards, the ability to feel into another person and empathize with them is a trait to be admired and cherished. It is, in fact, a real plus in the right environment.

BEYOND EMPATHY

I mentioned at the beginning of this chapter that not all empaths are the same. While we all share a deeper sensitivity to energy, there is a subset of empaths that I refer to as "old-soul empaths," and I count myself among them. These people have even more highly developed empathy. They also have what psychologist Sandra L. Brown, the founder of the Institute for Relational Harm Reduction, calls "super traits" of agreeableness, conscientiousness, and self-directedness. They are unusually optimistic, have a can-do attitude, an excellent work ethic, compassion, patience, and the ability to see the best in everything and everyone.

These individuals—75 percent of whom are women and 25 percent of whom are men—are the ones who uplift any endeavor in which they're engaged. Be it a marriage, a career, or a business, they are the ones giving 80 percent while those around them get by with 20 percent. Those with super traits become superhuman and end up being the person everyone in the family or on the job turns to when there's a problem. They are the CEOs of companies and families, deftly maneuvering among tasks and responsibilities with ease. They are the doctors and surgeons with great reputations for healing. They are the managers who make their employees shine. And they are the parents who head up the PTA while whisking their amazing children from activity to activity before heading out to raise money for a humanitarian cause they believe in. Everything in their lives seems easy, orderly, and put together.

In describing this group of people, Sandra Brown writes: "Super traits takes the concept of empaths a step further. While empaths are mostly focused on the trait of empathy, the theory regarding super traits is that these are *additional* traits that play along with empathy. They are hard-wired personality traits that will always be with someone, which act like a filter through which we read, or

misread, incoming red flags. Other super traits like toler-
ance, optimism about human nature, assuming others are
like yourself, warmth, openness, and being straight forward in disclosure—all of these play into the overall trait
of 'agreeableness' of which empathy is one factor."

It is my estimation that the super traits and hyperempathy displayed by old-soul empaths stem from the fact
that they have been here many times before. They have
learned the lessons of the world by living through centuries of hardship. They have had lifetimes of experiences,
and they know what it will take to make the world a better place—and their very being can assist in this. Old-soul
empaths can be very serious people because, on some level,
even at birth, they know what coming to the world means.
They know what they're getting into, and returning was
not a casual decision. No matter how necessary it was.

I talk about the return of a soul as necessary because
it's a journey that we all must take. The destination for
every one of our souls is enlightenment. It is nirvana. But
this state is not reached quickly or easily. Every soul must
learn the lessons of love and acceptance that are taught
through life experience. The soul must learn what it means
to be darkness and light, the abuser and the abused, the
weak and the powerful. It must experience all situations in
order to reach true enlightenment.

Before you incarnate in each lifetime, your soul signs
on to a soul contract that dictates the lessons that will
be learned in that lifetime. The events you experience are
all part of a plan to bring your soul closer to enlightenment. And a much higher vibration. As your soul moves
in that direction, you become more acutely aware of the
soul's journey.

We old-soul empaths account for about 0.5 to 1 percent of the population, according to spiritual teacher and

author Lee Carroll. We old souls all know each other when we meet. We're family. We "get it" about each other and about what's going on. No explanation necessary. There's a recognition. It's immediate. And it has nothing to do with where we grew up or where we went to college.

We see the world in a different way. We shine a light on the truth in things that are often outside the mainstream—energy medicine, homeopathy, spirit guides, and so much more. These are things that the majority of society has ridiculed and put down for centuries.

My old-soul friends and I often joke about our past lives—even though those lives were sometimes no laughing matter. In one former life, my Pilates teacher, Hope Matthews, and I were together on the same platform about to be hanged. And in another, I was drawn and quartered. In yet another, I was burned at the stake. When I mention this in lectures, I now often see audience members nodding their heads. My audiences these days are full of old-soul empaths.

We old souls have been the shamans, healers, midwives, tarot card readers, musicians, magic makers, and outliers of our communities for lifetime after lifetime. And in the patriarchal, fear-infused energy that has held down the planet Earth for the last 5,000 years or so, we've been punished, abandoned, or betrayed over and over and over again for what we know and what we believe.

Old souls are everywhere. And in all walks of life. We often use oracle cards and pendulums as aids when making decisions—though many times we keep this stuff hidden until we feel safe. We like to hang out in metaphysical bookstores, meditation centers, and ashrams. But we also recognize dark energy and avoid it when we feel it.

If you recognize yourself in the description of super traits but have a hard time with the rest of this definition, don't worry. Not every old-soul empath remembers past lives, nor do they all even believe in them. However, chances are good that you have a deeper understanding of the energy of the world than you may even like to admit.

EMPATHS AND VAMPIRES

All humans radiate energy, but empaths radiate a particular type of compassionate and understanding energy that can act as delicious life blood for energy vampires. While all empaths can become victims of energy vampires, old-soul empaths with super traits are especially attractive to vampires because of their high level of self-confidence and energy, and because of their belief in the goodness of all people. This is what makes them stay in relationships that drain them. Old-soul empaths believe—deep down in their heart of hearts—that everyone can change, so they stick with the vampires for years, even as their own health and self-confidence wanes.

Empaths who don't possess the belief that everyone is essentially good but who are still very sensitive to energy are often more highly skilled at identifying the red flags that suggest that someone is a vampire; as a result, they can steer clear or get out before the drain on their system becomes too severe.

That said, it is essential that all empaths understand the dynamics at play when it comes to energy vampires. Without this knowledge—and the information on how to heal from vampire encounters—you will never live up to your full potential. You will never be as healthy, energetic, joyful, or loving as you have the ability to be. Instead you will stay mired in the wounds of your past.

Chapter 2

THE WOUNDS
WE CAME TO HEAL

Not long ago I was in LaGuardia Airport in New York going through security. The TSA agent was a young blonde woman who seemed like she was in some kind of angry trance—not even making eye contact with the people whose IDs and boarding passes she was scanning. The agent next to her was equally disconnected. I wasn't even sure if he was working or if his station was open. He was that checked out. I travel a lot, and these two were, by far, the most disconnected individuals I've interacted with in a long time. Just going through the motions.

In my younger days, this interaction would have left me feeling bad—at least for a moment—wondering how I could somehow uplift these people or change the situation. Nowadays I know better. Most of the time.

I remember how back in the days when I had a medical practice—and before social media—I'd sometimes get nasty letters from patients whose needs I hadn't fulfilled. I even got one from a mother blaming me for her daughter's suicide because I hadn't accepted her as a patient years before. Each time I got one of these letters, I was crushed. It never occurred to me that it was impossible to be all things to all people. Or that the person writing the letter had an agenda that didn't include my well-being. I was out to save womankind, after all. These letters meant I had failed. I couldn't fix what was wrong. And so, I'd spend days afterward beating myself up about my lack of compassion, skill, love, understanding, etc. My mind spiraled: *What had I done wrong? Were they right? What could I improve? How could I do better?*

The same was true with the written feedback forms that were often shared with me after lectures for professional groups. Even though I would get 100 comments about how much people enjoyed and benefited from what I had shared, I would focus on the one negative comment about what a waste of time my lecture had been. Or maybe even how much they hated my voice or my outfit. That one negative comment would fester within me like a splinter in my heart.

While the vast majority of feedback I got—and still get—was positive, I am drawn to the one or two negative reviews like a moth to a deadly flame. Even though this is true for many people, it is especially true for empaths. That's because of the wounds and misunderstandings of our energy that we've experienced in this life—and for old-soul empaths, many lifetimes before.

SHAME AND GUILT

It's important to fully understand what I mean by wounds because these wounds shape our lives. They influence how we react in situations. They influence how deeply we believe in our abilities. They influence pretty much everything that makes us who we are. And those wounds come in the form of shame and guilt. These are, without a doubt, the two biggest obstacles to flourishing for highly conscientious old souls.

Many of us have been shamed for our social status, our body size, our age, our income level, how we talk, and where we've come from. These are all common themes. If you're living on planet Earth there is a 100 percent chance that you will be shamed about something by someone. In many ways, the social pressure to be perfect has never been greater. Girls as young as eight years old are worried about being too fat. And 11-year-old athletes are being yelled at by the parents of the other kids on their team for something they did during a youth hockey game. Phrases like "Big boys don't cry" and "What are you, a pussy?" or "Don't you think you're getting a little pudgy?" can—in a highly sensitive and conscientious person—plant the seeds of self-abuse and self-hatred. Boys who have been shamed tend to act out, while girls turn their shame inward, often creating depression, eating disorders, or perfectionism.

While the shame we experience from our acquaintances can be tough, the truly damaging shame is that which we get from the very people who are supposed to protect us. Dr. Mario Martinez, in his brilliant book *The MindBody Code*, points out that all tribes wound their members with three archetypal wounds: shame, abandonment, and betrayal. Your tribe might be your family, your profession, your religion, or any other group you have relied on for support and with which you identify. Tribes the world over use these wounds to keep their members "in line." The wounds themselves stem from expectations of how things "should" be.

These expectations are formed by the dictates of society on the large scale (country, heritage, and so on) and small scale (religion, activity groups, and so on). A classic example of these expectations is heterosexuality. The intense shame and guilt experienced by a homosexual child in a family that was dead set on heterosexuality as the one and only way could create extreme feelings of self-hatred and self-doubt.

The expectations of the family can also be shaped by the wounds that the members of the family experienced. Think about it. If your mother was a studious child who was shamed because she was no fun, she might do everything in her power to protect you from this shame. She would enroll you in activities that seemed fun without regard to your true nature.

Holding people accountable to living by these expectations by using shame, guilt, and abandonment is extremely effective because these feelings are so painful to experience—especially for an empath who feels the disappointment and judgment of others so acutely. And then makes the mistake of thinking that something is wrong with her.

When we are shamed as children for being who we really are, we begin to doubt ourselves. We internalize the belief that something is inherently wrong with us. And this leads to self-punishment, self-blame, and even self-hatred. If you grew up in a household that rewarded you only for doing what they wanted you to do—and shamed you for what you were naturally drawn to—you may have grown up with a lot of self-doubt. And not much self-trust.

A LIFETIME OF WOUNDS

The wounds you experience in childhood shape your entire life—most of the time without you even realizing it. They form the belief system from which you operate, and the vast majority of these beliefs are not even conscious. About 90 percent of them—and the subsequent behaviors that come from them—are programmed into us before the age of seven. These all operate below the radar, influencing our biology and circumstances automatically. They were downloaded before our own intellects came on board, which is about the time that the secondary teeth come in. These unconscious beliefs and behaviors were handed down to us from our parents and their parents before them. Think about it. If your parents believe that an essential part of you, like your ability to see into other worlds, is wrong, they didn't come up with this on their own. Likely their parents handed this belief to them.

So when we are told that something is wrong with us, we feel ashamed of ourselves, certain that we are flawed and unworthy of the best that life has to offer. When that happens, we become driven by an insatiable need to prove our worth. We have an unending need for approval from others to feel okay about ourselves. Our personalities, including our super traits, and the bonds we form with others are driven by our wounds, not our strengths and magnificence. The underlying beliefs about our worth in the world stem from the wounds we have experienced. These beliefs and the relationships we build based on them lead to living in an environment likely to be filled with anger, guilt, blame, and judgement—all of which keep us feeling stranded in disconnection and worthlessness.

Until I started working on healing my own wounds, I hadn't realized just how powerful they were in creating the life I have led. They are the reason I have worked so passionately to open women's eyes to the true power of their own bodies. They are the reason I have been able to stand powerfully on my own. But they are also the reason I have been in relationships that don't suit my best self and situations that have led me away from my soul's calling.

In a recent session with a skilled healer, I was guided to identify where my beliefs about life had originated. After calling in my guides and angels—and his—for this healing session, this healer put his hands on my abdomen. Age 12 came up over and over again. He "saw" me crying beside a fence and said he felt an enormous amount of pain from that time. And he was right. When I was 12, I developed plantar fasciitis, astigmatism, classical migraines, and the onset of painful periods. My period pain was so intense that I had to leave school every month for years. And later on, I even had to scrub out of surgery. The healer I was working with helped clear some of the pain from my body, but the true source of it was unclear—until later that night when a dream opened my eyes to a very powerful wound.

In the dream, it was the present day and I was with my family, all of whom were there with their spouses and children. My father was also there (even though he died when I was 28). I had spent the night in a house that wasn't familiar to me. And in the morning, I got up because I had to catch a train and a plane to do some kind of work. My sister-in-law brought me my suitcase. But it was empty. I couldn't find any of my clothes—all of which had been put in drawers the night before. I was running out of time and really had to catch that train. So I asked my family members to help me find my stuff. But everyone ignored me. I kept pleading with them: "Please help me. Won't somebody please help me?" And that's when I woke up in tears, feeling my 12-year-old sadness in every cell of my body. And for a few hours, I just stayed with the emotions that this dream had brought up. And cried and cried.

Clearly the healing had loosened the lid on the jar of my unconscious. I realized that at the age of 12, as the black sheep of the family, I had made the decision that no one was going to help me achieve my goals because they were so different from that of the other family members. I was a straight-A student in a family that was far more interested in athletic performance and mountain climbing. Once when I asked for a quiet place to study (translating Caesar's *Gallic Wars* from the Latin), my father said, "We can't all rearrange our lives for you." Of course, had I wanted to become an Olympic athlete, like my sister, they would have moved heaven and earth for me. My mother drove my sister to ski races every weekend—10 hours each way—while I made dinner for the family during her absence. I never questioned this arrangement because we were all so proud of her. She was the youngest girl on the World Cup circuit back then. An amazingly gifted athlete. Still is. She brought our entire family a lot of positive regard.

After that dream, it was clear to me that I had decided when I was 12 years old that the only person I could really trust was myself, and that no one was going to help me. If I was going to fit in and be valued, I had better find out how to provide value and service to others. Like cooking and baking. And cleaning up. Or giving impromptu harp concerts to guests—whether I wanted to or not. That is how I lived my life for decades. Meanwhile I was hiding much of what I really believed. I learned how to fit in to almost every situation presented—no matter whether it fulfilled me or not. And that included lots of camping trips in the rain, climbing mountains with a heavy backpack on, being cold and wet on ski slopes, being a golf caddie for my mother, and trying desperately to learn golf and tennis while being made fun of by my siblings and parents, who were all naturally gifted athletes. For many, my childhood sounds ideal. For me, it was, in many ways, torture. Still, it was all great preparation for medical school and surgical training. And I know that my soul chose it. Without that background, I would never have had the stamina or discipline to do the work I've done so far.

So how did the situation with my family lead to my adolescent symptoms? If you think about adolescence, this is the time when people become interested in finding out the answers to questions like, "Who am I?" and "Why am I here?" For me, these questions led to the answers "I'm not good enough" and "I don't fit in." They led me to doubting myself and feeling like I needed to hide who I really was. Shame, guilt, and anger—even though I don't remember feeling angry back then—created the headaches, eye problems, and menstrual cramps.

Please remember, the pain I was releasing during that dream and after was the pain of a wounded 12-year-old, not the adult I am now. My family supported me in many ways, including paying for and driving me to music lessons, paying for college, and buying me a concert grand harp. But pain is pain. And it's stunning to realize that at some level, that grief-stricken 12-year-old who decided she couldn't trust anyone had been running my life in major ways for decades. Pain comes to the surface when you have a strong enough ego and enough maturity to handle it. Clearly it was time for me to trust more and release the past.

The wounds of my lifetime—and all my previous lifetimes—led me to become who I am, but it was time to let them go. That is the healing that I had come to earth to experience in this lifetime.

THE WOUNDS OF OUR ANCESTORS

Dealing with the wounds from our own experiences is hard enough work, but that isn't where the wounding ends—or, actually, where the wounding begins. Trauma can be passed genetically from grandparent to parent to child. When a trauma happens, a chemical change occurs in our cells. This chemical change attaches to our DNA and changes the way our genes function. In his book *It Didn't Start with You: How Inherited Family Trauma Shapes Who We Are and How to End the Cycle*, Mark Wolynn, director of the Family Constellation Institute, teaches that the changes in DNA that are the result of trauma are designed to protect us and our children by making sure we're prepared to deal with the original trauma. But what if we or our children are constantly bracing for trauma that no longer exists? If we grew up in a war zone, we'd likely learn to duck and take cover from bombs and gunshots. And then our children would be more likely to automatically be overreactive even when they are safe.

The trauma of our parents, grandparents, and great-grandparents can live in our anxious words, fears, behaviors, and unexplained physical symptoms. This is known as inherited family trauma or secondary PTSD. Even if the person who suffered the original trauma has died, or the story has been forgotten or silenced, memory and feelings can live on. This has been demonstrated rather dramatically in the grandchildren of Holocaust survivors who often had nightmares of death camps and starvation even if they were shielded from their grandparents' history and never even knew about what happened.

As Wolynn writes, "These emotional legacies are often hidden, encoded in everything from gene expression to everyday language and they play a far greater role in our emotional and physical health than has ever before been understood."

As an empath, you are here to transform not only the wounds from your lifetime but also the legacy of pain. You are here to end the pain.

Chapter 3

VAMPIRE-EMPATH RELATIONSHIPS

With our natural proclivities for taking care of others, along with the wounds we empaths have endured—and the work we have done to gain acceptance—it is no wonder that we are desirable prey for people who feed off the energy around them. This is especially true for old-soul empaths because we believe in the goodness of people. Deep in our hearts and souls, we see the best in everything and everyone. We can see the potential of another person from a mile away, and we're naturally drawn to helping that potential come to fruition. We're the enthusiastic, loyal, can-do cheerleaders who fan the flames of love and light—even when others can't see it. We come into the world with centuries of healing wisdom.

The natural tendency of an empath is to want to uplift situations. To improve people's lives and to provide others with opportunities that very often we ourselves didn't have.

And so we find ourselves naturally drawn to the "fix-er-uppers" of humanity—the ones who need our light. Helping feels good. In fact, it's one of the true joys of being on earth. There is nothing more fulfilling than watching an underdog come from behind and win, especially if it's because that person has finally found someone who sees and supports them. For example, I met a man this spring who went from being in a foster home to becoming an internationally known boxer. The turning point came when a man saw him at practice and said, "There's some-thing about you. I see something in you. I want to help." That was the key that turned the whole thing around. We know that having just one person believe in us and see us can make all the difference in whether or not we manifest our dreams.

When a relationship works for mutual benefit—whether that's creating a home, a family, a business, or being of service to those in need—an alchemical magic happens. The unbridled healing energy of two or more people working in harmony for good creates a third energy that is greater than what each person could do individu-ally. This is the quantum healing energy that Jesus was talking about when he said, "Whenever two or more of you are gathered in my name, there will I be also."

However, on the other end of the spectrum are non-supportive relationships. This is where the problem comes in. If we happen to get in a relationship with someone who isn't in the relationship for healthy reasons, our wounds become activated. Because of our belief that we have to offer something of value in order to be accepted, we strive to make others happy—even at the expense of our health and our sanity. Since we don't believe that anyone will value us for who we really are, we don't dare share our vulnerabilities in relationships lest we be rejected. I once had a man refer to me as "bulletproof" compared to other women. What he meant by that was that I didn't seem to have any needs or vulnerabilities. How very wrong he was. I just had built up a lifetime of skill in hiding those needs. And getting them met by myself.

As I mentioned in Chapter 1, all empaths are seen as prey, but it is the old-soul empath who often becomes embroiled in long-term relationships with a vampire because we tend to believe the best about everyone, assuming they are like us. We simply can't see the red flags that other people often pick up on. So, we idealize people and relationships in ways that aren't realistic or healthy. A good illustration of the fairy tale we are drawn to is the iconic scene in the movie *Jerry Maguire*, in which Jerry (played by Tom Cruise) arrives in his beloved's living room during a support group for divorced women—and tells Renée Zellweger's character how his success has meant nothing because she wasn't there. And then he utters, "You complete me." And every woman in the place swoons, wishing that some guy would say that to her.

So many empaths have an unhealed inner child who has been trying to win love through service and sacrifice for most of our lives that we tend to take on too much responsibility for the health of a relationship. We're so used to over-giving that if someone gives 25 percent compared to our 75 percent, we feel like we've finally arrived in relationship nirvana. OMG—he put down the toilet seat. He must love me.

When we don't feel good about ourselves, our relationships are driven by the unmet needs of that inner child. I'll be returning to this issue again as I address the wounds we empaths need to heal within ourselves. We give what we desperately want to receive. Being alone with our wounds is not an option—at least until we recognize them. So we're apt to stay overly long in relationships in which we over-give and under-receive, especially when the relationship looks good from the outside. After all, there's certainly a societal benefit to appearing normal.

This can be an issue in any nonsupportive relationship, but it gets especially devastating when we're in relationship with an energy vampire.

A FORCE TO BE RECKONED WITH

Energy vampires, as I noted earlier, feed on the life force of others. Unlike a relationship in which the dysfunction may be based on incompatible personalities, the dysfunction in an energy vampire relationship is based on careful manipulation.

Energy vampires keep energy coming their way by masterfully playing into the wounds of the people around them. The empath, then, is a special target for the energy vampire because the wounds in their lives go so deep, which means that they are easier to manipulate. The energy vampire hooks into the empath using what I call "malignant intuition." By this I mean that they have an unerring sixth sense about the wounds of an empath. They know exactly what the empath has been longing to hear their entire life. Vampires make a beeline for the wound—and then love-bomb the empath with precisely the kind of attention and recognition they have been longing to experience since birth . . . and maybe even for lifetimes. To an empath, this kind of attention is a welcome relief. Ahhh . . . someone who finally "gets me."

But that's not the case at all. The vampire simply knows the empath's weaknesses and uses them to their own advantage. They are fully aware of what they are doing.

Now I know what you may be thinking, *Really? Everyone who drains my energy is doing so on purpose?* Well, no. There are people who are inadvertent energy drainers. These people share some of the same characteristics as full-fledged vampires, but they aren't fully on the spectrum of personality disorders we're talking about.

These negative people may not be conscious of their impact on others. Here's how you can tell. You're with a Debbie Downer friend, and you find a caring and compassionate way to tell her that her energy is bringing you down. And it's a regular pattern that bothers you. Her response will tell you everything you need to know. If she's mortified, owns this critique, and is willing to admit that your point of view is valid, you're not dealing with a vampire. But if she starts to cry and run for the victim role—or gets angry and tells you what's wrong with you, you have your diagnosis. A normal person will own their own stuff and work to fix it. They will not make you wrong for sharing your truth. In fact, doing so will make the relationship stronger. People of good will have the ability to experience true remorse and the desire to change—just like you. Vampires don't.

We'll discuss this more in Chapter 5, when we dig deeper into the characteristics of energy vampires, but just know that true energy vampires know exactly what they're doing. They are incredibly skillful at assessing your weaknesses and taking advantage of them.

Where the confusion begins is that in a vampire-empath relationship, the vampire is initially very supportive of your goals and dreams. Because the vampire is often so adroit at initially supporting you in your efforts to heal, you begin to trust them and their judgment. You feel as though you've finally found someone who gets you, wounds and all. You relax and let your guard down, and perhaps you let them into your life deeper than you've allowed anyone else. Their hooks are now in you.

This is when they begin to criticize you and use their inner knowledge of you to discredit the people, things, and dreams that are your passions—all of which they initially supported.

At one point in my career, I had a colleague who was incredibly supportive and helpful with my work. This was extraordinarily rare at the time, because as a holistic physician I was always waiting for the next shoe to drop and for the "authorities" to punish me in some way for my beliefs and approach to healing.

Over time, however, this individual used her intuition to tell me what was wrong with just about everyone who came into my life—personally or professionally. I initially found this very confusing, as she had been a gifted intuitive whose guidance had been very helpful. But after a while, I came to realize that if I didn't cut off the friendship completely, I would eventually end up walled off from the world entirely, and the only person who would be interpreting my reality for me would be her. She even tried to come between my daughters and me. But I saw the pattern. It was exactly how abusive men isolate their victims. This often happens so slowly—and under the guise of caring for you—that you don't realize what is going on when it's happening.

VAMPIRES IN YOUR LIFE

So take a look at your own life. How many of your friends or, worse yet, family members, call you only when they want something or have a problem? Notice how these same people never call you just to check in on how you're doing. It's a one-way street, with all the attention and energy going to them, not you.

Take notice of who calls you for advice, to complain, or to simply talk on and on while you listen. This is a pattern that went on for decades with me until it finally dawned on me that these individuals never called unless they wanted something. Here's an example. I'd get a call from an old friend and think, *Oh, how nice. They're reaching out because they care and want to acknowledge me.* My little inner child would get excited: *Oh, goodie. They're checking in. They really care about me.* And then the other shoe would invariably drop when I quickly realized that the only reason they called was so I'd give a quote for their manuscript, make an introduction for them, or give them some healing advice about a health problem they or an acquaintance was having. The thin veneer of caring about me went away very quickly. With nothing given in return.

Before we empaths realize what is happening and stop the behavior, we often find ourselves freely sharing our wisdom, time, and resources with those who call us during nights, weekends, and just about any time it is convenient for them. We give freely because that's our nature. And we fan the flames of their potential. Lovingly. And when they hang up the phone, we, at first—maybe for years—feel good about ourselves for being valuable to them. But over time, we find that they are not there for us. And very often they don't even follow our advice. And nothing changes. They just wanted a hit of our energy, or a voice on the other end of the line telling them what they already know. Or else they want us to do something for them.

Those who call and never change very often have a lot of drama in their lives. They feed off it. And create it. That's why, at first glance, they are so exciting to be around. Have you noticed that? I was recently visiting an old friend and we were talking about the friend who first introduced us decades ago. I'll call her Joan. As we shared our stories about Joan, we both realized that each of us had spent hours and hours over the years listening to her dramas, trying to help her solve her problems. But she never changed. She simply went from drama to drama while we tried to help her out financially and socially. Finally we both saw the pattern and withdrew. Comparing notes was eye opening. You too? Yes. Me too.

Here's the thing. If there were no drama, the energy vampires would have to look at the spiritual side of life. But they are afraid of it. Trauma and drama are comfortable. This is why the mainstream news cycle is so negative. It's familiar and comfortable. And it sells product. It is also addictive. There is always something to fix. Something outside yourself to focus on so that you never have to look inside—the only place where your true power lies. The place where no one else can do the work for you.

When there is nothing more to fix, the only thing you have left is the Divine, by whatever name you choose to call it. And vampires don't want to go there because their approach to life works for them. They genuinely don't think anything is wrong with them. Why would they need to look inside? The goodies are all outside—money, sex, power. In a subsection of his classic book *Without Conscience: The Disturbing World of the Psychopaths Among Us*, Dr. Robert D. Hare, an expert in this field, writes about why nothing seems to work with the worst of these characters: "And here is the crux of the issue: Psychopaths don't feel they have psychological or emotional problems, and they see no reason to change their behavior to conform to societal standards with which they do not agree."

Empaths, on the other hand, generally have a very solid relationship with God and their faith in a Divine Source. We feel bad for those who don't, and we're eager to share that deep and abiding faith with another. But they don't want to do the work of contacting that Divine within. They'd rather just get a hit of our energy to keep them afloat until the next time. And if we don't recognize our own role in keeping this drama going—which is attempting to be their Higher Power by being available all the time and having all the answers—then we risk losing ourselves and enabling them to stay stuck. Do you see this happening in any of your relationships?

STUCK IN RELATIONSHIP

If you're in a relationship with an energy vampire, the question is: Why don't you get out? Why don't you speak up and protect yourself?

As I mentioned, many empaths do get out. They see the problems and ditch the vampire pronto. But for those who don't, there are two main reasons. First, you are naturally compassionate and caring, so you may simply miss the red flags. That can happen if you're not fully paying attention to your intuition and the circumstances around you. And second, your wounds have created in you a powerful desire to be accepted and an overwhelming belief that you shouldn't hurt other people's feelings. And for old-soul empaths, there's a third thing that keeps us stuck: We truly believe that our love and caring can heal other people—in this case, the vampire. And though we may see the red flags, we believe that things will be different with us—that those other people who hurt the vampire just didn't have the skill and compassion that we have.

While our initial response to their inevitable ill treatment of us is anger, hurt, and disappointment, we quickly squelch these natural feelings and replace them with guilt—something we learned to do in the past, either way far back in another lifetime or in childhood. Or, more likely, both.

We make the mistake of thinking that energy vampires are as sensitive as we are. We don't want to risk hurting their feelings, so in order to protect them and their feelings—and because we're so darn good at solving problems in all the other areas of our lives—we keep giving them our energy and draining ourselves rather than risk standing up to them, standing up for ourselves, and owning how angry, hurt, and disappointed we really feel. And then ending the relationship.

We take on the responsibility of trying to convince them to get help and to change their ways. But this is a dead-end street, because they don't change. What has to change in every single relationship with an energy vampire is *you*. You need to finally *be done* and get out of the relationship. I know this is hard to hear, especially for those of you who have invested so many years and resources into making the relationship work, but the sooner you give up on them and choose you, the healthier, happier, and more effective you will become.

One of my friends, who has recently been recovering from a marriage to an energy vampire, was telling me about how her life has changed since she finally left him. As part of her healing, she recalled a past life in which she was old and in a cave. Her entire tribe was abandoning her. And almost every member of the tribe had been a child that she, as a midwife, had brought into this world. Talk about abandonment and grief. In her current lifetime, her family called her weird from the time she was a little girl for her interest in meditation, yoga, Sanskrit, nutrition, and healing dance. Her skills in those areas are off the charts. However, her self-trust and self-esteem were always on the low end of the spectrum given her background. Plus, she has a lot of self-sacrificing energy and shame as a result of taking vows of poverty and chastity in many monastic past lives that involved self-flagellation and brainwashing about her worthiness as a woman.

This is what had made her a sitting duck for an energy vampire despite her super traits and multiple Ph.D.s. She had come into this life believing that she was unlovable, so when she met this handsome and charming man who started the relationship love-bombing her and paying a great deal of attention to her, she was all in. When they met, he had just had a windfall of money from the sale of a family business—a business he didn't build. It was just inherited money. And then, after they were married, he immediately came down with one excuse after another about why his business ventures always fell through. He was, as they say in Texas, "All hat and no cattle."

Because she didn't know about the deadly dance between old-soul empaths and energy vampires, she did everything in her power to uplift him and make him successful. She paid for him to go through a bunch of business trainings and also paid for many of his recreational trips—all the while hoping that this would make him happy and successful. After all, he was tall and handsome and had so much potential. While she worked 80-plus hours per week at three different jobs, he contributed almost nothing. And yet, he accused her of overspending.

After 19 years of this, she found herself suffering from adrenal fatigue, insomnia, thyroid problems, sore breasts, and very low self-esteem. She also began to doubt her own sanity.

The lack of self-worth and need to be accepted and loved that many have makes us a perfect target for energy vampires and the darker parts of human nature. This is true not just in our most intimate relationships, but also in work settings. One woman I worked with had a job as a personal secretary for a very wealthy and successful man. Though she was well-educated and did her job beautifully, he continually asked for more. And when she'd say, "These additional hours are not in our agreement," he'd reply, "But sweetheart, you run my entire life. What would I do without you?" And that would appeal to her conscientiousness: *Oh, wow. He really needs me. I'm making a difference!* She couldn't manage to create a boundary between her private life and work because he always violated them. One of her co-workers—who had watched this play out with her predecessors—once said to her, "If you're still here by December, I'll know you're crazy." When she finally left—because of failing health—her boss's final words were not "Thank you so much for doing an amazing job." Nope. They were "Will you miss me?"

We also see this dynamic a lot in spiritual relationships. As mentioned before, old-soul empaths are drawn to spiritual teachings and gatherings. And many have been drawn to various gurus. I actually experienced this myself when I became involved with a meditation movement that was just getting started. The organization tried very hard to enroll me as a teacher. I even set up a bunch of lectures in my hometown. But I soon saw that this organization—and others like it—expected a huge amount of unpaid service. The only person who ended up with any resources at all was the guru. I'm not talking about individuals who have enjoyed a fruitful experience with a spiritual organization that has uplifted them and made their lives better. This is certainly possible. But I've seen far too many gurus of all stripes—some religious, some not—who dupe unwitting empaths into supporting causes that end up draining the devotee of her self-esteem, money, and time. This happens over and over again with charismatic leaders who pretend that they have a direct line to God, when in truth, God is not outside of us in some prophet form. God is inside. That's what we've come to live and teach by example.

The vampire—whether a man, a woman, a lover, a co-worker, or a guru—survives by draining the life force and resources of the empath, who too often ends up sick, confused, broke, and emotionally devastated. All because the wounds of the empath were used against them. And they didn't know it until it was too late.

SUCKING YOUR LIFE'S BLOOD

To understand what I mean by "survives by draining the life force," we need to look at the term *narcissistic supply*. This is a game changer once you understand the dynamics in a vampire relationship. Narcissistic supply is the "blood" that manipulative people suck out of empaths. Vampires manipulate others for this narcissistic supply, which comes in the form of attention, money, sex, and status. There's an old saying: "Talk about me good. Talk about me bad. Just talk about me." Vampires tend to suck all the oxygen out of whatever room they are in, because there's some kind of abyss inside that can't be filled. But that doesn't stop them from trying.

Vampires will often pick a fight if things are going too smoothly, just to get a hit of energy. It doesn't matter if the energy is good or bad. That's what narcissistic supply is—directing energy, attention, and money toward themselves, which they do very skillfully.

Sometimes the energy drain in the direction of the vampire is so striking that you literally feel like falling asleep when you're around them. I was visiting the home of a very successful woman a couple of years ago. On the surface, she had everything. A magnificent home, an incredible global business, all kinds of outside help. I was excited to meet her.

While I was sitting at lunch, looking out the window at her beautiful gardens, I was suddenly overcome with sleepiness—like that poppy scene in *The Wizard of Oz*. I had to fight to keep myself awake. When lunch was finished and we went into the living room to visit, all I wanted to do was lie down on the rug and sleep. I'm serious. It was that bad. I kept biting my lip and pushing my nails into my palm to try to stay awake. I even pulled up the woman's astrologic chart and did her tarot cards. Anything to stay awake and keep the conversation going. Happily I was with a friend who was having the same reaction. Though we had planned to spend the weekend, we realized that we had to get out of there. So we hatched a plan to gracefully excuse ourselves.

I've had that same thing happen on several other occasions with individuals who, on the surface, were charming and accommodating. But below the surface, something else entirely was going on. That's because vampires can be chameleons in relationships, often knowing how to give you "just enough" attention or improvement in behavior to keep you hooked. They will tell you exactly what you want to hear to keep you sucked in, feeding their narcissistic supply.

When you threaten to end the relationship, the vampire will often become extremely accommodating and commit to change. They might even be willing to go see a therapist. And you think, *Oh, my God, he gets it. Things are going to be better.* But that's not true. What actually happens is that the vampire may put in just enough effort to get you to stay—usually by charming you with his words and promises to change. But no substantive behavior change ever comes. And if you stay, this can be disastrous for your health and your life. One of my patients put it this way after finally divorcing a vampire: "I swear, if he had given me just a crumb of affection or attention, I would have stayed. Thank God he didn't. Because if I had stayed, I know I would have died of breast cancer. I'm pretty sure I was headed in that direction."

Chapter 4

THE HEALTH RISKS OF UNBALANCED RELATIONSHIPS

Have you ever seen a couple that just didn't seem to make sense? A stunningly attractive man with an overweight, puffy, tired-looking woman? Or the other way around? I'm guessing you have. And you may have found yourself wondering, *What does he see in her?* Here's the thing: These are vampire relationships. The person who looks like a million bucks is a vampire, and the person who looks drained and sick is a highly sensitive person— and the vampire's narcissistic supply. She is the source of his life energy. It's literally like a transfusion is occurring in which the vampire is draining the empath. Individuals who can see and sense energy can even observe this as energy cords between the two people.

Once you begin to understand the dynamics of a vampire relationship, you'll begin to observe how the vampire—when he or she doesn't have a source of narcissistic supply—suddenly becomes like a black hole. They have nothing to offer. That "life of the party" person you always enjoyed being around is reduced to a boring, complaining individual with nothing to offer. One of my colleagues told me that she can always tell when her former vampire husband has a new girlfriend—he suddenly cleans up, works out, and looks like he's glowingly healthy. But when he's without a source to plug into, he looks old and tired. And is extremely boring to be around. This is also when he's apt to call her. Just to get a little "hit" of her energy. She no longer takes the calls.

This relationship of an energy vampire to their source of supply is akin to what happens in nature when a parasitic plant such as mistletoe overtakes an elm tree. Mistletoe grows within the vascular system of a tree and extracts nutrients and water from that tree for survival. This is obviously not good for the health of the tree. Depending on how much the mistletoe takes over, it may actually end up killing the tree. It is the same for those in relationship with a vampire. If an empath has a strong constitution, eats well, and takes care of him or herself in other ways, then she or he may well be able to withstand the energy drain imposed by the vampire. For a while.

But over time, it takes a toll—and that's when the effects of being with an energy vampire are not just emotional or about feeling drained. The disparity in appearances is the first step toward a whole array of physical ailments that are often just as painful and dangerous as the psychological ones. In my experience, I've seen that highly sensitive people who stay in vampire relationships eventually end up suffering from health issues like adrenal fatigue, chronic Lyme disease, thyroid disorders, an inability to lose weight, irritable bowel syndrome, diabetes, breast cancer, and so-called mystery illnesses and autoimmune disorders that don't respond well to conventional medical treatments. In fact, I'd say that in my decades of experience on the front lines of women's health, the root cause of an individual's health problems is *very often* that they are involved with a vampire—either at home or at work. And until that is addressed, no exercise, meditation, yoga, or nutritional program is going to permanently help them regain and maintain their health. That's because every time they put a deposit in their health bank account—by going on a yoga retreat or a juice cleanse, or getting a massage—the vampire in their lives just drains them as soon as they return home.

One of my colleagues, who has a Ph.D. in nutrition, is also a yoga teacher, and has given workshops internationally on healthy lifestyles and diets, was married to a vampire for 20 years. And despite all of her knowledge and healthy behavior, she still suffered from debilitating adrenal fatigue and weight gain—despite an enormous amount of regular exercise. She took many trips to exotic places for health retreats. And I always wondered why she traveled so much. Turns out it was the only way she knew to survive. Because every time she returned home—all glowing and healthy—the same old vampire tactics drained her within a few weeks. And she was right back where she started.

In a recent phone conversation, psychologist Sandra L. Brown reported that fully 75 percent of the women who come to her retreats to recover from narcissistic abuse suffer from autoimmune disorders and the kinds of things I mentioned above.

THE CHEMICAL CAUSE OF ILLNESS

So let's look at how physical health issues come about in a vampire relationship. On a basic level, the stress of having to deal with constant disappointment, negativity, trying to "fix" someone, deception, and all the other things that go with a vampire relationship can lead to physical symptoms because of the chronic, unrelenting release of stress hormones in the body. It is very well documented that people who are exposed to chronic social conflict experience dysregulation of the immune system, thereby increasing their susceptibility to all kinds of infectious diseases including so-called autoimmune disorders. According to WebMD, 75 to 90 percent of all visits to primary-care doctors are for stress-related complaints. I can certainly attest to the validity of this from my own years in practice.

In their groundbreaking publication *Stress in America: Our Health at Risk*, released in 2012, the American Psychological Association surveyed Americans in the East, Midwest, South, and West. And though there were differences in the stressors listed in every region, relationship and family stressors were the second most common stressors after money throughout the entire country. If you were to drill down on exactly what these relationship stressors were, I have no doubt that you'd find that an inordinate amount of the relationship stress results from trying to get a vampire to take responsibility for his or her actions—or cleaning up after them.

So what happens when someone is under unrelenting stress? The adrenals produce a stress hormone known as cortisol. Under normal circumstances, small amounts of cortisol suppress inflammation and provide you with the ability to get out of danger. However, when cortisol levels remain high, the body actually begins to produce inflammatory chemicals known as cytokines. And these are associated with a whole host of symptoms, including headaches, weight gain, digestive problems, joint pain and swelling, fibromyalgia, arthritis, and eventually diabetes and heart disease. You see, chronic cellular inflammation is the root cause of almost all chronic degenerative disease, including cancer and diabetes.

Right now many people with so-called autoimmune disorders are being told that their real problem is a virus, like Epstein-Barr. And while there is a level of truth to this, it is an incomplete explanation. There are millions of viruses around us and in us all the time. In fact, they are an innate and often helpful part of what is known as our "microbiome"—the trillions of bacteria and viruses that live in and on us all the time—and which are responsible for keeping us balanced and well. The only time that a virus such as Epstein-Barr (of which there are hundreds of types, including all the herpes viruses) becomes a problem is when your immune system is off balance because of chronic stress and cortisol levels that are too high! This is when your body isn't able to keep them in check naturally.

How often have you found yourself popping NSAIDS (nonsteroidal anti-inflammatory drugs) on a regular basis to ease the pain resulting from chronic cellular inflammation? Got a headache? Pop an ibuprofen. You get the picture. The problem with masking the pain of cellular inflammation with drugs is that it never addresses the real problem: the vampire causing you to live with perpetual stress that not only increases cellular inflammation on its own, but also encourages you to indulge in behaviors and dietary choices that increase cellular inflammation in their own right.

Chronically high cortisol levels also wreak havoc with hormone levels. Libido often goes away when someone is under stress. And libido, which we often think of as just sex drive, is actually a subcategory of something much broader—something known as "chi" in traditional Chinese medicine. Chi is a good measure of one's life force. When there is excess cortisol, estrogen gets metabolized into an additional stress hormone—especially during perimenopause. Excess cortisol also results in high insulin levels and swings in blood sugar. The end result of all that is an insatiable craving for sweets or alcohol, weight gain, and inability to get a good night's sleep. All of this tends to show up big-time at midlife, a time when our souls cry out to be heard. And when we find ourselves far less able to tolerate—at least physically—the manipulation of a vampire.

COGNITIVE DISSONANCE AND STRESS

Back in 1957, Leon Festinger published a book called *A Theory of Cognitive Dissonance* that put forth the theory that we humans seek consistency in our beliefs and attitudes in any situation where two cognitions are inconsistent. The theory also states that a powerful motive to maintain cognitive consistency can give rise to irrational and sometimes maladaptive behavior. We all hold many beliefs about the world and ourselves. When they clash, this results in tension that is known as cognitive dissonance. Over time, cognitive dissonance in and of itself produces chronically high cortisol levels in the body and subsequent chronic inflammation.

Festinger's theory of cognitive dissonance arose out of a study of a cult whose members believed that the earth was going to be destroyed by a flood. He investigated what happened to the cult members when the flood didn't happen—particularly those who had given up their homes and jobs to work for the cult. He found that the fringe members were very likely to admit that they had made fools of themselves and just "put it down to experience," whereas the hard-core committed members interpreted the lack of a flood as evidence that the righteousness of the faithful had prevented the disaster.

Dissonance can be reduced in three ways. First, individuals can change one or more of their behaviors to lessen the dissonance. An example would be the cognitive dissonance of a smoker who continues to smoke, knowing that smoking can cause cancer. In the first way to eliminate the dissonance, you accept the facts and change your behavior accordingly. In this instance, you'd have to give up smoking. The second way to reduce the dissonance is to get some new information. A committed smoker might point to cases of individuals who have smoked all their lives and never had a problem. The dissonance would be reduced within the individual by the new belief that smoking doesn't cause problems in all cases.

And then the third way to reduce dissonance is to decrease the importance of one's beliefs. So, in the case of smoking, the smoker could say, "Oh well. I really enjoy smoking. And I'm going to live for today and enjoy my cigarettes."

In this example, every time the smoker encountered someone with smoking-induced cancer (or even thought about it), they would experience the stress of cognitive dissonance—and they would have to fight for the justification they've chosen.

The same situation applies to an individual with super traits who is in a relationship with a vampire. These people absolutely believe in their heart of hearts that people can change, that love can heal anything, and that they can figure out how to help their partner. They experience the stress of cognitive dissonance every time the vampire does something hurtful, especially after years of "fixing." When faced with lies, manipulations, and aggression, the individual with super traits will experience stress—and then fight for justification in staying in the relationships. You may recognize this in yourself. Your partner puts you down and you find yourself hanging on the one memory of the time he was nice to you at Christmas. Or the time he complimented you and told you you looked good. Or the fact that he's really good in bed.

Indeed, Sandra Brown has found evidence of brain changes in those who have lived with cognitive dissonance for years. Women describe not only anxiety and depression, but also brain fog and the inability to make decisions or to trust themselves. These oh-so-effective women who excel in every other area of life develop executive function disorders and lose the ability to think straight.

And it isn't just Sandra who has seen this evidence. Recent studies reported in the neuroscience literature using brain scanning technology have shown how people who have lived with cognitive dissonance have brain changes similar to people who have been diagnosed with PTSD.

That's some pretty compelling evidence that shows just how life-changing this kind of emotional abuse can be. It also helps explain why so many of the women in Sandra Brown's retreats suffer from autoimmune disorders. In a 2017 article published in *Arthritis & Rheumatology*, researchers found that PTSD and more general trauma were associated with a higher risk of developing the autoimmune disease lupus. The risk was three times higher for women with PTSD, and twice as high for women who had experienced trauma.

This is just one of numerous studies that has looked at the effect of psychological stress on the development of an autoimmune disease. In 2008, *Autoimmunity Reviews* published an article called "Stress as a Trigger of Autoimmune Disease" that noted, "Recent reviews discuss the possible role of psychological stress, and of the major stress-related hormones, in the pathogenesis of autoimmune disease. It is presumed that the stress-triggered neuroendocrine hormones lead to immune dysregulation, which ultimately results in autoimmune disease, by altering or amplifying cytokine production." They concluded from these reviews that treatment of autoimmune disease should include stress management.

HEALTH CARE TODAY

Back when I first started my medical practice in the 1980s, the term PMS was relatively new. None of my colleagues even believed that it existed. Noticing that PMS responded beautifully to lifestyle changes, I became fairly well-known back then as a doctor who could help women who were experiencing monthly mood swings. Every single one of these women responded well to dietary change, B vitamins, exercise, and other stress-reduction techniques—for a while. And then, inevitably, almost none of them were able to sustain the lifestyle changes after three months. I wondered why. And over the years, I found that in nearly every case, the woman was either working with or living with a vampire. It was no wonder she couldn't sustain her healthy lifestyle. The root cause of her problem had never been diagnosed. It was the same with chronic pelvic pain. After all, it wasn't until the late 1980s that my profession even acknowledged the link between sexual abuse and pelvic pain. We doctors are trained to look for the physical cause. Back then my colleagues would say to me, "We only see normal women," suggesting that the problems my patients were experiencing were "all in their heads."

That same cognitive dissonance runs throughout the health-care system. The overarching belief that runs the system is this: Germs, bad luck, or bad genes are the cause of illness. It has nothing to do with your diet, your relationships, or your life. But don't worry. There is—or soon will be—a drug that you can take for your condition. The fact that adverse pharmaceutical drug reactions and medical mistakes are the third leading cause of preventable death in the United States isn't even addressed. We're just trained to wait for the next big pharmaceutical breakthrough.

I've been a doctor long enough to see that so-called mystery illnesses which weren't taken seriously by conventional medicine two decades ago have now become "real" and finally taken seriously only because a company has developed a drug to treat the symptoms. Fibromyalgia is a perfect example. Twenty years ago, fibromyalgia and chronic fatigue were dismissed out of hand when women showed up suffering from this condition. Now there is a drug that can be prescribed but which doesn't even begin to treat the root cause of the problem.

Fibromyalgia, like all illnesses to some extent, is a good example of how illness is actually a learned physiological response to specific stressors. As Dr. Mario Martinez points out, most illnesses involve a learned pattern which, at the beginning, has a positive function. Let's take the inability to sleep soundly, which is so common in those suffering from chronic fatigue and fibromyalgia. Lack of sound delta wave deep sleep results in widespread cellular inflammation, in part because deep sleep is absolutely essential for metabolizing stress hormones. Martinez suggests that being hypervigilant and learning to be a light sleeper may well be a highly adaptive strategy when you are living with a threat of some kind—like sexual or physical abuse. Later, in adulthood, when that childhood threat is no longer relevant, the body's stress response and the impact on the psychoneuroimmunologic system are still there. And over the years, this sets the stage for fibromyalgia and chronic fatigue.

Instead of looking at the root cause of a dysfunctional immune and nervous system, however, modern medicine always manages to find yet another drug, and then prescribes it "off label"—meaning that it can be given for purposes other than originally intended—at least until the drug company funds a study that suggests that the drug works for "fill in the blank." That is how Prozac and the other SSRIs have become popular as "treatment" for PMS and menopausal symptoms. All this despite their addictive nature and the fact that they don't actually resolve the issue at its root cause, which is the hormonal effects of stress on the immune, nervous, and endocrine systems.

Many people know—in their guts—that the majority of chronic health problems are the end result of emotional and psychological stress in their lives. It's very easy—and culturally encouraged—to ignore this information given that the health-care system largely dismisses the unity of the mind and body.

Genetic Determinism

One of the biggest pieces of misinformation in health care today is the notion that an individual's health is determined by his or her genes. And that no matter what we do, we're victims of our genes. Diseases "run in your family." There is nothing you can do about it. These are the cards you've been dealt. But this isn't necessarily true.

Dr. Bruce Lipton, developmental biologist and author of *The Biology of Belief*, points out that only about 10 percent of what happens to your body and your health is in any way related to your genes or your family history. That means that 90 percent of what happens to you—including how your genes get expressed—is determined by your environment. This is the science of epigenetics. And the most important part of that environment is created by your beliefs, most of which you are not consciously aware.

Dr. Mario Martinez, founder of the Biocognitive Science Institute and author of *The MindBody Code*, points out that many Tibetan monks have diabetes that cannot be explained by their diet or lifestyle. In general, these monks eat healthfully. Yes, some are obese. And yes, many eat carbs. But they don't overeat or overload on sugar, and yet they still have an unusually high rate of diabetes.

The work of Dr. Martinez and others suggests that the development of diabetes is intimately connected with their belief systems of forgiveness and loving-kindness. More on this in a moment. According to biocognitive theory, what we believe and what our culture teaches us has more impact on our health than our diet and lifestyle factors. A great example of this is the research of Dr. Becca Levy of the Yale School of Public Health who studied 660 people over the age of 50 in an Ohio community and found that those who had positive perceptions of getting older (which were already in place in their teenage years) conferred seven extra years to their lives. That's right—just the belief that growing older had positive aspects resulted in a longer life. And that was true even for those who smoked, were lonely, were obese, had high blood pressure, and never exercised. In other words, belief trumped all other measures we associate with longevity.

Dr. George Solomon, a pioneer researcher in the field of psychoneuroimmunology, taught that the immune system has morals. It responds in a positive way to righteous anger—the kind of anger that is natural to feel when your own innocence or that of another is threatened. Our immune systems won't let us get away with bypassing our more "difficult" emotions if we want to remain healthy. Anger is, after all, the appropriate response when you are being abused. Suppressing it is a health risk.

Let's go back to the Tibetan monks (who, you might say, are role models for what we empaths think we should be). The Chinese have done a huge amount of damage to the Tibetan culture and its people. They have raped, pillaged, and destroyed temples. The natural response to this is anger and rage. But the monks have been taught not to feel that anger and instead to send love to their enemies. This sends a signal to the body: "I don't want to feel anger. I'm beyond my anger." The other factor with the Tibetan monks comes from their culture. The pioneering work of Dr. Daniel Goleman, author of *Destructive Emotions*, notes that the Tibetans don't have a word for emotion. In their world, thoughts and emotions are the same thing. So you could say that culturally, they are not well-versed in the language of emotions and how they feel in the body. The monks learn to send empathic joy to those they should first feel angry with if they want to remain healthy. They literally "sugarcoat" their anger. And diabetes is the result. Dr. Martinez, who has worked with many Tibetan monks, said that they are trained not to care about their physical bodies either and are focused only on spiritual matters, like returning to Buddhahood, where a body isn't necessary.

So how does sending loving-kindness to those who have harmed you—without first feeling your anger—result in stress that can lead to illness? When you do this, you experience the following biochemical cascade. The physical body confirms the desire to send only loving thoughts by producing large amounts of a chemical known as endorphin (akin to morphine). It numbs pain, and prevents you from feeling things you don't want to feel. The problem is that chronically high amounts of endorphin adversely affect glucose metabolism over time. And type 2 diabetes is the result.

I've known several highly sensitive people—who attract vampires like a magnet—who have high blood sugar despite an almost perfect diet. And in all cases, these individuals sugarcoat everything they say and do; they appear to be literally unable to feel their anger. They instead go right to forgiveness and compassion.

Tendency to Gain Weight

One of the most striking things I've observed in relationships between vampires and sensitive souls is the disparity in their tendencies to gain weight. Vampires are often (not always) far more able to maintain a healthy and attractive weight. And it often seems effortless. One vampire, when I bemoaned my inability to lose weight, once said to me, "I just stopped eating dessert for a couple of weeks and lost ten pounds." I know what he was thinking: *I see the problem. You just lack discipline.* But nothing could be further from the truth, especially for old-soul empaths. We often have discipline to burn. And still, until we can learn how to stop taking on the energy of others and draining our own, we're apt to do two things: (1) be attracted to sugar, carbs, and/or alcohol; and (2) keep weight on no matter what we do—even if we stop eating carbs.

Empaths tend to put on weight easily, in part because the weight acts as "protection." Hence the weight distribution in empaths is almost always in the middle of the body—that dreaded "apple shape" with excess belly fat that is a risk factor for cardiovascular disease and diabetes. This weight distribution acts to protect the solar plexus, the area in the body associated with self-esteem and personal power. Until you learn how to create healthy boundaries and shore up your self-esteem, you're not likely to achieve a healthy weight.

THE POWER OF OUR THOUGHTS AND BELIEFS

So when we look at the health of a person who is active as the source for a vampire, we have to look at the beliefs that they hold about themselves and their relationships. As discussed before, these beliefs—which are reinforced in a vampire relationship—start to be formed in childhood when we are shamed and betrayed, forced into hiding who we truly are. And remember, toxic shame produces an inflammatory chemical known as IL-6—one of the cytokines.

The link between adverse childhood experiences and illness is a growing field, with more and more studies being done each year. In one of the largest studies—the famous Adverse Childhood Experiences Study (acestudy.org), which started at Kaiser Permanente in the weight-loss clinic—it was discovered that there is a direct relationship between the number of adverse childhood experiences (e.g., divorce of parents, a mentally ill parent, a chronically ill parent, or an abusive parent or relative) and the number of times the individual used the emergency room, filled prescriptions, or even died prematurely.

Among people who have been exposed to major psychological stressors in early life, there is increased vulnerability to vascular disease, autoimmune disease, and premature death. And these tendencies show up as a person gets older. Remember that empaths are highly sensitive by nature, and so it may not take a truly major psychological stress to create future vulnerability.

Researchers suggest that childhood stress somehow gets "programmed" into an immune system cell known as a macrophage through epigenetic markings (epigenetic meaning the way the environment affects the way a gene is expressed).

Cells then become endowed with proinflammatory tendencies, which manifest as exaggerated cytokine responses to challenges and decreased sensitivity to inhibitory hormonal signals. The study abstract, which was published in *Psychological Bulletin* in 2011, states: "The model goes on to propose that over the life course, these proinflammatory tendencies are exacerbated by behavioral proclivities and hormonal dysregulation, themselves brought about through exposure to childhood adversity."

In real life, what that means is that childhood stress—in susceptible individuals—may give rise to excessive threat vigilance (always feeling like the worst is going to happen or that you're not worthy, and thus vibrationally attracting it), mistrust of others, poor social relationships, impaired self-regulation, and unhealthy lifestyle choices. Hormonally, early stress also can result in altered patterns of hormonal and nervous system regulation. So, in essence, adverse childhood events favor a pro-inflammatory environment both inside and outside the body! And this drives the body toward pathology unless the pattern is changed.

It's fascinating that in Sandra L. Brown's experience working with survivors of vampire relationships, fully 75 percent of the women come from normal homes with no evidence of neglect or abuse. But I am willing to bet that if you dig a little deeper, you'll find that these super-trait women have some dings in their self-esteem resulting from either a past life or their childhood.

There is evidence to suggest that one of the true risk factors for immune disorders, e.g., what is called autoimmunity, is the childhood experience of having our survival linked to conforming to expectations that are actually a violation of who we really are. Dr. Gabor Maté, a physician and expert in stress and childhood development, says that every single one of his patients has struggled with emotional repression as a coping style. Moreover, not one has ever been able to answer yes to the following question: "When, as a child, you felt sad, upset, or angry, was there anyone you could talk to—even when he or she was the one who had triggered your negative emotions?"

In his magnum opus, *When the Body Says No*, Maté cites study after study demonstrating the effect of particular stressors on the physical body that directly and powerfully express how immunity behaves. For example, a study of African American vs. Nigerian men showed that though both groups have the same number of potentially malignant cells in their prostate glands, fully six times as many African American men actually develop prostate cancer. Same genes; completely different environment.

Researchers, including Maté and Dr. Lawrence LeShan, make the argument that those of us who twist ourselves into pretzels to please others or who otherwise suppress our own emotional needs in service to others are at particular risk for developing immune system problems such as Hashimoto's thyroiditis, fibromyalgia, chronic fatigue, etc.

The reason for this is that the immune system confirms what we already believe—as I already suggested above. If you believe that you are worthy and lovable, your immune system will confirm that. If, on the other hand, you are depressed and feel worthless, you will be far more susceptible to everything including the common cold. A fascinating study from the University of Pittsburgh in which volunteers had their throats sprayed with cold viruses found that those who were the most likely to actually get sick were the ones with the weakest social networks and support systems. On the other hand, those who had four or more different social groups with whom they interacted regularly were far less likely to get sick—despite everyone being exposed equally. The work of Dr. Bruce Lipton, author of *The Biology of Belief,* points out that it is the membrane of the cell that is, in fact, the brain of the cell. And cell membranes are connected with each other so intimately that a single thought courses through the body with lightning speed—creating biochemical changes in our cells that are the result of the quality of our thoughts.

When we believe that we aren't worthy or valuable, our lives are saturated with a particular type of chronic self-denial. We too often end up controlled by energy vampires who relegate us to a subordinate position. This can leave us feeling disempowered and helpless. And sooner or later, we get sick.

Countless studies have confirmed the unity of body and mind, despite the fact that conventional medicine is still based on an artificial split between the mind and body. The conventional medical "drugs and surgery" approach (though amazingly wonderful when dealing with trauma) leads people to believe that their state of health is determined by bad luck, bad genes, or a deficiency of some drug.

But in truth, your state of health is very intimately connected with your core beliefs. And the quality of your day-to-day emotions stems directly from those thoughts. As I've already stated, about 90 percent of our beliefs aren't even conscious. And the vast majority of them are negative. But our conscious mind is the place where our hopes and dreams reside. So our job, as empaths who want to make the biggest healing impact we can and live our best possible lives, is to be willing to do the work necessary to upgrade our beliefs and thoughts—and feel and release any emotions that haven't been fully felt and named.

PART II

HEALING FROM DARKNESS

Chapter 5

RECOGNIZING YOUR VAMPIRE

So now that you understand the vampire-empath relationship—and the terrible results you can experience as a side effect—let's get into the good part: how to fix it. The first step in this is learning how to recognize a vampire. This will help you see the people in your life for who they are—and it will also help you spot a vampire before you get in relationship with them next time. So let's delve a bit more deeply into their personal characteristics— what makes someone a vampire and how to see their manipulation tactics before you become entangled.

DIAGNOSING YOUR VAMPIRE

It is only in the past 25 years or so that energy vampires have been clearly identified by the mental health profession. That is why so many of them have so successfully continued to manipulate their families and society in general. Make no mistake—energy vampires are often charming and charismatic. You often can't take your eyes off them (until you realize who they really are). They know exactly what to say to whom. And when to say it. And they are masters at getting others to do their bidding. My friend Bob Palumbo, a Ph.D. psychologist with 35 years of experience, says that some are so very charming that even he, with all of his experience and knowledge, can be taken in. It's important for all of us to know this.

Labels for the behavioral patterns of vampires include sociopaths, psychopaths, narcissists, borderline personalities, or people who are prone to antisocial behavior, but all of these personality types can be grouped under the term Cluster B. The *Diagnostic and Statistical Manual of Mental Disorders (DSM-5)*—a publication of the American Psychiatric Association—notes that Cluster B individuals are characterized by dramatic, overly emotional, or unpredictable thinking or behavior. This designation includes antisocial behavior (sociopathy), borderline personality disorder, histrionic personality disorder, and NPD (narcissistic personality disorder).

The antisocial ones are liars and cheats and have recurring problems with the law. They disregard their own safety or the safety of others. They often engage in repeated violation of the rights of others. They won't take responsibility for their actions and are often aggressive, impulsive, and even violent.

Those with borderline personality disorder engage in impulsive and risky behavior such as unsafe sex, gambling, or binge drinking or eating, but can also be unbelievably compelling and charming. They often threaten self-injury or say they are going to commit suicide, especially if you don't give them what they want. Far more women than men are considered borderlines. They operate with what is called intermittent reinforcement—the most difficult kind to deal with. Sometimes they are there for you. Sometimes they are not. This inconsistency is maddening and makes you feel crazy. The good men who have been in relationship with borderline women often end up like empty husks by the side of the road—having had a borderline suck their lifeblood from them.

One of my colleagues recently told me that when she was growing up, her mother often threatened to kill herself if her daughter didn't do her bidding or disappointed her in some way. Imagine the impact of this on a young child. Being made to feel as though your behavior had the power to keep your mother alive or kill her. How often have you heard the phrase "Please don't do that, it would kill Mom"? This is borderline territory.

At our hospital, the psych department calls the more advanced borderlines "frequent flyers"—some of them coming to the emergency room more than 200 times per year saying they feel suicidal. Then once they are admitted, they begin to demand special attention and special meals.

Borderlines are masters at engaging in "splitting behavior," pitting one person against another. They often have ongoing feelings of emptiness. (I've dealt with borderline patients who get pregnant year after year because after the baby is born, they feel "empty.") In Buddhism, this kind of person has been called a "hungry ghost," meaning that they have no inner sense of self. They have an abyss inside that can't be filled no matter how much you love and attend to them. They have frequent intense displays of anger. And are very manipulative.

Individuals with histrionic personality disorder also constantly seek attention. They are often excessively emotional, dramatic, or sexually provocative. They often speak dramatically with strong opinions but with no facts to back them up. They are easily influenced by others and have rapidly changing emotions. They have excessive concern about their physical appearance and often think that their relationships are closer than they are.

Vampires with narcissistic personality disorder have fantasies about power, success, and attractiveness. They crave fame and recognition. They don't recognize the needs and feelings of others. They feel superior to others and act entitled.

They often exaggerate their achievements and talents. I once had an acquaintance whose résumé stated that she had graduated from art school with an MFA (master of fine arts). I happened to know that she had dropped out of the program in her sophomore year. When I brought this to her attention, she said, "Well, it felt like I had that degree." Huh? That would be like me saying, "Well, it felt like I went to medical school and got an M.D."

Narcissists require constant praise and admiration. They are often arrogant, and they believe that they are special. And they can be unbelievably physically attractive and, because of this, tend to get the equivalent of full service at self-service prices wherever they go—especially in their younger days. (There's an old adage that states that narcissists don't age well.) They have unreasonable expectations of favors and advantages, often taking advantage of others who, depending on their own self-esteem, often feel blessed just to be in the narcissists' presence—at least initially. They also are envious of others or believe that others envy them.

Some can also be miserly, with tight control over budgets. They may also have an inability to discard old or worn-out objects. They can also be morally inflexible.

It is interesting to note that the ratio of male to female vampires is about 4:1, but fully 20 percent of all people (male and female) have vampire characteristics or are full-blown Cluster Bs. That's one in five people, and each one of those directly and adversely affects five people. That's 60 million people in the U.S. alone. In her book *The Sociopath Next Door*, psychologist Martha Stout writes, "1 in 25 ordinary Americans secretly has no conscience and can do anything at all without feeling guilty." That's 100,000 psychopaths in New York City alone.

Robert D. Hare, Ph.D., author of *Without Conscience: The Disturbing World of the Psychopaths Among Us*, has worked in the field of criminal justice and psychopathy for decades and has published dozens of academic articles on the subject. He and his colleagues spent many years developing a highly reliable diagnostic tool called the Psychopathy Checklist for clinicians and researchers which is now used worldwide to help distinguish with reasonable certainty true psychopaths from those who merely break the rules.

He reminds us that most criminals are not psychopaths, but many of the individuals who operate on the shady side of the law but remain out of prison are indeed psychopaths. A major part of Hare's decades of work has been an attempt to identify them. As he writes in *Without Conscience*, "If we can't spot them, we are doomed to be their victims, both as individuals and as a society." Then he gives the all-too-common example of the convicted killer who is released on parole—and immediately kills again. Society asks, "Why was such a person released?"

In response, Hare writes, "Their puzzlement would no doubt turn to outrage if they knew that in many cases the offender was a psychopath whose violent recidivism could be predicted if the authorities—including the parole board—had only done their homework."

Many psychopaths are white-collar criminals who bilk the public of millions, yet, even once convicted, spend very little time in jail or in changing their ways. This is beautifully articulated by Drs. Paul Babiak and Robert Hare in their book *Snakes in Suits: When Psychopaths Go to Work*. White-collar psychopaths are the kind of brilliant masterminds who steal the life savings and pension plans of thousands, like the CEOs of Enron, a company that went from being worth billions to declaring bankruptcy overnight. A company that encouraged all of its employees to invest their pension plans in its stock while the principal masterminds sold theirs and got out with millions before the bottom inevitably fell out. Want to see what this looks like in living color? Watch Alex Gibney's 2005 documentary *Enron: The Smartest Guys in the Room*. Absolutely mesmerizing. Psychopathy in action.

It doesn't matter whether someone is a Cluster B vampire or a full-on psychopath—either way, they are an enormous public health problem that has largely gone undiagnosed and unrecognized by both individuals and society in general, including the mental health profession and the court system.

Keep in mind that there is a continuum with Cluster B people just like people with autism. Some people on the autism scale have a little Asperger's syndrome and are fully capable of living fulfilling and independent lives. On the other end of that spectrum are individuals so disabled they cannot live without full-time care. Likewise, some people have narcissistic traits that you can learn to live with once you can recognize the behavior. This is where those inadvertent energy drainers come in. They are just at the very bottom of the spectrum. But as you start moving up the scale, you get to the true vampires—the full-blown psychopaths. The Cluster B designation is useful because there is such wide overlap among all of these characters.

You needn't spend any time splitting hairs over these diagnoses. It won't help you. If you're currently in relationship with an energy vampire, I can almost hear you saying, "But he means well. He just had a difficult childhood." First of all, this is not always true. And even if it were, most people who grow up in difficult situations do not become energy vampires. The vampire knows exactly how to play the empathy card to keep an empath hooked in. As I noted before, the tendency of an empath is to make excuses for the behavior of a vampire. Instead, what you need to realize is this: What every vampire has in common is covert aggression and manipulation for personal gain. They are fighting for the upper hand. Period. End of story.

BORN THIS WAY

Sigmund Freud, the father of modern psychotherapy, suggested that the types of problems we see in Cluster Bs resulted from childhood trauma and the denial of it. But this simply isn't true. Modern brain-scanning techniques suggest that many are simply born this way.

In a study published in a 2013 issue of the *Journal of Psychiatric Research*, a team of German researchers using modern brain-scanning technology studied the brains of 34 volunteers, half of whom had been diagnosed with narcissistic personality disorder (NPD). The part of the brain that was examined was the cerebral cortex, the outermost layer of the brain that we associate with the "higher" social centers in humans. This is the part of the brain that regulates self-awareness, self-determination, and self-control. One particular part of the cerebral cortex is associated with empathy—the part of humans that allows us to feel both emotionally and logically what others are feeling. In those with NPD, this part of the cortex differed from those with normal empathy.

When compared to people unaffected by NPD, people with NPD have unusual cerebral cortex thinness in the region responsible for empathy. And interestingly, the authors also found that the degree of "missing" empathy matched the degree of thinness present in that region of the cortex.

Functional MRI studies, which were published in 2013 in *Frontiers in Neuroscience*, have also shown marked abnormalities in psychopaths in a number of brain areas associated with empathy and the ability to care for the well-being of others. An fMRI study of affective perspective-taking in individuals with psychopathy—imagining another in pain—does not evoke empathy.

In a 2010 study published in the journal *PLOS ONE*, a team of researchers from the University of Southern California used modern brain-scanning technology to examine brain activities in a group of volunteers during specific tests. And also during a period of rest. Though all the volunteers were normal with no diagnosis of NPD or other mental conditions, they did exhibit varying degrees of NPD traits on standard personality testing. After reviewing the results of the brain-scan activity, the authors found that narcissistic traits were linked with unusual levels of activity in a part of the brain associated with self-absorbed thinking. They also found diminished activity in the part of the cerebral cortex associated with impulse control, which would increase the likelihood of poor decision making in those with higher narcissistic tendencies.

Though a vampire might have experienced childhood trauma, that trauma does not explain their lack of compassion and lack of a conscience. Most people who've come from traumatic backgrounds have a conscience and behave in ways that exhibit good character—knowing right from wrong. And of course there are vampires who have grown up in loving homes who still manipulate to get their way. A recent article in *The Atlantic* titled "When Your Child Is a Psychopath" features an 11-year-old girl (and many other examples) who was raised by a loving family along with six other siblings. Starting at the age of six, she began fantasizing about killing people, drawing murder weapons and practicing on her stuffed toys. Soon enough, she tried to strangle her little brother. She is one who will grow up lacking compassion and conscience.

In cases like these, the conscience that is supposed to develop around the age of three or so simply doesn't. For example, one of my friends had a terrible experience when she was seven. Her brother, who was nine at the time, locked her in a shed at their house and watched as his friends—who he had lined up for the occasion—raped her. Her mother, who was worried about what the neighbors would think, never validated any of this and refused to punish the brother, thus creating a deep and enduring wound my friend has worked to heal throughout her life.

Unfortunately, in traditional psychotherapy we often use childhood trauma as an excuse for the vampire's current behavior. For example, you might hear, "He's just like that because his mother was an alcoholic and he is in denial about his pain." The works of George Simon, Jr., Ph.D., author of *In Sheep's Clothing*, and Sandra L. Brown, M.A., author of *Women Who Love Psychopaths*, convincingly argue that this is definitely not the case. Dr. Simon illustrates that true denial is quite rare. And it happens as a defense against extreme emotional pain. Here's an example based on Dr. Simon's work. Imagine that you and your loving husband of 40 years are out walking in your neighborhood and having a wonderful day. Both of you are in great health. Then suddenly your husband collapses from a stroke and is taken to the hospital where he's put on life support. You go from enjoying a walk with the love of your life to seeing him on life support within a couple of hours. Imagine that the doctors then come in and tell you that the damage to his brain from the stroke is so severe that he is essentially brain dead and he will never wake up and be conscious or able to breathe again. The enormity and suddenness of this loss is so great that you go into denial to protect yourself. You sit with your husband. Hold his hand. And talk to him. Even though the medical staff tries to convince you that he can't hear you. That is denial. And it's a perfectly reasonable psychological defense in that situation.

Now let's take the case of a class bully who walks down the halls of a school and routinely pushes students' backs so that they drop their books. The hall monitor calls him out on it. And he looks around and says, "Huh? Like—what do you mean? I didn't do anything." Is that bully in denial? Absolutely not. He knows exactly what he was doing. He just keeps doing it because he is a thrill-seeking individual whose brain empathy circuits aren't very well formed. Once he knows he can't get away with this behavior, the behavior will be extinguished. But as long as he knows that someone is going to think he is deeply wounded and in denial, why stop? He can keep this kind of thing up for a lifetime. Without consequences. Because so many well-meaning empaths will think he just needs more love and understanding.

Or what about the abusive spouse who pushes his wife up against a wall or hits her? He excuses his behavior by saying, "She was on my case all day. I finally snapped. I couldn't take it anymore." The abuser knows full well that what he did was wrong. But to avoid the consequences, he puts the blame back on her. She made him do it. That doesn't make any sense. She was not in his brain connecting the motor cortex with the musculature of his arm.

In his book *Character Disturbance: The Phenomenon of Our Age*, Simon outlines how manipulative characters really work and the way in which we as a society enable them. He points out the misused psychological terms that keep everyone stuck: So *acting out* really means *acting up*. *Denial* is actually *lying*. *Defensive* should be replaced with *combative* or *aggressive*. And what empathic people call *shame* is actually a vampire's discomfort for being *exposed*. In truth, these characters could use a little healthy shame—as in be ashamed of their behavior—which they are not. What we call *passive aggressive* is really *covert aggression*. *Codependence* should be replaced with *dependence* or *abuse*. What we call *help* should be replaced with what it really is: *chasing* or *enabling*.

Supportive therapy, love, and empathy doesn't help them. Not a bit. In fact, it makes matters worse. Those who have been led to believe that love and caring will heal everything would do well to remember that even saints like the famous Padre Pio of Italy sometimes refused to serve Mass to those who came to see him if he deemed that they weren't worthy.

Now, I know what you're thinking: *But what about neuroplasticity? Can't they change?*

We all know that it's possible for the brain to change over time. After all, new studies on neuroplasticity—the ability of the brain to change—have shown that learning new things keeps increasing the size and number of cells in our hippocampus, the area of the brain associated with memory. Women in their 70s who consistently try new things—like dancing or taking up new physical activities or learning a language—have brains that are nearly as sharp as the brain of a 20-year-old.

However, neuroplasticity and change are contingent on one thing: *willingness.* You will never get *any* sustainable and positive changes in your brain unless you, yourself, are willing to change something. The Cluster B person has to *want* to change. And the chances of that happening are basically zero. So, yes, it's technically possible, but it is highly, extremely, overwhelmingly, tremendously, crushingly improbable. Remember, they are born this way. Just as you didn't choose to be born as an empath, they didn't choose to be born with their personality. So the goal here isn't to judge them as evil or try to fix them. It is simply to avoid them, or at the very least, set up very healthy boundaries, and save yourself.

RECOGNIZING A VAMPIRE

The first step in saving yourself is seeing the problem. So here are the common characteristics of energy vampires. And remember, this is a continuum. Some people are full-out vampires. Others have certain vampire traits. All use manipulation to get their needs met.

They are often charming, good-looking, charismatic, and outgoing. They often have hypnotic eyes that draw you in to whatever they are saying. They may hold high positions in government, business, religion, the military, and medicine. Think CEO of a Fortune 500 company. Or prominent political figure.

Charismatic vampires tend to surround themselves with followers who hang on their every word, just like the guru situation I mentioned in the previous chapter. And these minions often do the bidding of the vampire, just like the flying monkeys in *The Wizard of Oz*. In fact, when you begin to wake up and call the vampire out on his or her behavior, the minions will begin to attack you, and you constantly feel as though you have to defend yourself and get them to listen to your side of the story. (This never works, by the way. Just work on yourself.)

They often have a complete disregard for right and wrong. Character is defined by how you behave when no one is looking, but vampires often commit their biggest crimes when no one is looking, and then turn into model citizens when the camera is on them—like a politician who weeps with compassion on camera but lines his pockets with taxpayers' money when the cameras aren't rolling.

Looking good is one of the most cherished values of a vampire. So confronting any weakness in them or suggesting an area of improvement is often met with stonewalling or rage.

Their self-esteem is derived from personal gain outside of themselves—how they look, what kind of house they live in, what kind of car they drive.

They can be pathological liars who are often excused by society because they are so good at manipulation. They minimize ("I didn't hit her that hard"), outright lie ("I never said that"), or tell half-truths—leaving out salient details. These master manipulators are so often enabled by society that they can, quite literally, get away with murder. As Sandra Brown points out, "The world appears to be tilted in their favor."

They refuse to take responsibility for their behavior. It's always someone else who is "doing it" to them. In a recent discussion, my friend clinical psychologist Dr. Bob Palumbo told me, "It's very easy to diagnose a borderline. They screw you over, rip you off, commit whatever transgression, and then they blame you for it." Bingo.

They are predators who prey on empaths by hooking them with "sob stories" such as "My wife had an affair and left me. And now I never see the kids."

Vampires are often bored, so they like to keep things stirred up. Hence they are often very flirtatious, fun, and entertaining. So fun, in fact, that the fear of losing out on all the fun and glamour that surrounds them tends to keep more introverted empaths hooked. Compared to their lives, your own life can seem so ordinary and unexciting. You don't want to lose out.

A vampire from my past always started every conversation with "You won't believe what happened while you were gone." Then she'd launch into a soap opera of drama that was very entertaining indeed. But over time, I saw that this was just her M.O. for getting narcissistic supply and attention. Once this kind of constant drama had left my life, I reveled in the newfound peace of my existence. In fact, the level of peace was so profound that my business partner and I commented on it regularly—for a couple of years. Always saying, "Wow, isn't it an incredible relief to not have to deal with all that drama all the time."

One way vampires bring drama into their lives is through health concerns. It is estimated that anywhere from 25 to 30 percent of the patients in a primary care practice use illness to get their emotional needs met. They have absolutely no interest in getting well because they get so much attention during their doctor visits. Dr. Mario Martinez puts it this way: "Illnesses are easier to treat than the fear of coming out of the illness and doing what you have to do without the illness."

Full-on narcissists can be hypersexual and very good at sex. They are also exquisitely seductive and often very attractive. They are rarely monogamous and often have affairs. And they will, unfortunately, toss you aside in a heartbeat without a second glance when you are no longer providing them with the supply they need. Imagine being married to a vampire for 20-plus years, and suddenly waking up to what's been going on and demanding a change. Most likely, you'll be stunned when the person you've loved and sacrificed for (certain that they will eventually change) not only doesn't change, but instead finds a new mate (source of narcissistic supply) within a month or so. This can be devastating to the empath, who wonders, *Did he ever really love me?*

So when you're looking at your relationships and your interactions with someone whom you suspect to be a vampire, look for the use of these common manipulation tactics:

- Being aggressive or covertly aggressive to get their own way.

- The need to always "win." They won't take "no" for an answer, and if you try to resist, they wear you down until you give up.

- Lies that portray them in the best light,
  no matter what the situation—or their real
  part in it.

- Super competitiveness and fighting for the
  upper hand, making sure to always display
  their "power."

- No straight answers, even to a simple
  question. For example, they might answer the
  question, "Can I count on you to pick up the
  groceries tonight?" with "You know how tired
  I get after work."

- Blaming others for their own hurtful actions.

- Laying on guilt trips in order to make you
  feel bad.

It can be hard to identify your vampire because often you become mired in the day-to-day details of the lies and the guilt trips. You spend your time trying to handle the negative consequences that come at you every day, so you don't have time to see the big picture. But to recognize that someone is a vampire, you often need to take a step back and look at their behavior patterns, not simply behavior incidents. It can be hard to make this shift—to reframe your perspective of someone—but 10,000 feet up is sometimes the best place from which to see their true nature.

As you fight your natural inclination to stay in a relationship and "fix" the other person, please do remember that vampires don't have a moral compass or a conscience. They lack true compassion and true remorse. They think they are perfect. They often exhibit vengeful behavior, are frequently angry, lack remorse, and are incapable of intimate relationships. They often exploit others through deceit. I know that this is difficult to accept, but they know exactly what they are doing. They are *not* in denial at all.

They are masters at using specific interpersonal maneuvers or tactics to gain advantage over you. Once you recognize how they work, you are far less likely to be victimized by them.

Chapter 6

PUT YOURSELF FIRST

In his book *In Sheep's Clothing*, Dr. George Simon writes, "The most fundamental rule in human engagement is that the aggressor sets the rules. This is because, once attacked, weakened in position, or emotionally on the run, any victim of aggression (including covert-aggression) is always scrambling to establish a more favorable balance of power." Or, as the old cliché goes, "The best defense is a good offense."

So now that you've learned to recognize your vampire, it's time to get yourself on the offensive—and that's what the rest of this book is about. Tips, techniques, and tactics that will put you in control of your own life and your own relationships.

In the case of dealing with an energy vampire, the first thing you have to do is admit that there's a problem. It's often hard for empaths to accept that there are people who aren't filled with love and light. There really are predators who lack character, empathy, and compassion. The sooner you accept this, the safer and happier you'll be.

So then, once you've accepted this truth, what do you do to avoid being the narcissistic supply for someone? Let's start at the very beginning: recognizing the relationship.

ASSESSING YOUR RELATIONSHIPS

To understand if you are in a relationship with an energy vampire, there are two things you need to know: (1) how to identify an energy vampire, and (2) your own likelihood of being in relationship with an energy vampire. In short, you need to know how to correctly assess the character of others and yourself. You must recognize and correctly identify manipulative tactics. You also need to be highly aware of the aspects of your own character that make you vulnerable to manipulation.

We covered, in depth, the tactics and traits of an energy vampire in the previous chapter, so if you need a refresher on that, go back to page 76 and read that again. All I'll say here is that there are a couple of phrases you've probably heard that can help you decide if you're dealing with an energy vampire:

- "By their fruits you shall know them."
- "If it walks like a duck and quacks like a duck, it's probably a duck."

These phrases can help you form an idea about someone's character. Remember, the manipulator is fighting for something—control, narcissistic supply, attention, status, the upper hand. Don't pay attention to what he or she is saying. Be on the lookout for the tactic that they are using to win. Look to their behavior, not their words.

Now we get to the harder part—knowing yourself. If you identified with the discussion of what makes an empath in Chapter 1, then you are well on your way to understanding that you could be in a relationship with an energy vampire.

But keep in mind that the most powerful leverage a vampire has is the character of the victim. He knows how she will likely respond to his tactics. So the more you know yourself—and your own vulnerabilities (which may be strengths in all other areas of life except with a vampire)—the less power energy vampires will have.

In addition to the super traits of conscientiousness, loyalty, and the patience of a saint, Sandra Brown has identified a number of character styles that make women more vulnerable to manipulation. While Brown's research and work have focused solely on women, these same traits make men similarly vulnerable. The resource list at the end of this book will be as helpful for men as for women. I've listed the character styles below with some self-assessment questions to see if these apply to you:

- **Extroversion and excitement seeking:** Do you find that you often get into relationships with people who are extroverted and exciting? Does the idea of being in a "comfortable" relationship seem boring to you?

- **Relationship investment:** Do you give great emotional, spiritual, physical, and financial investments to all your relationships—not just your intimate ones? Do you often feel as if you are giving 80 percent while the other people give only 20 percent?

- **Attachment:** Do you have the capacity for deep emotional bonds? Do you form powerful bonds with people quickly? Do you form bonds that make you feel beholden or desirous to do anything asked by the other people in your relationships?

- **Competitiveness:** Are you unlikely to run out on relationships? Do you stand your ground and fight for relationships to continue? (Keep in mind, we're not talking about codependence here.)

- **Low harm avoidance:** Do you assume that you will not get hurt? Do you see others as you see yourself and assume that they feel the same way?

- **Cooperation:** Are you the can-do person who rolls up your sleeves enthusiastically when there's a task to be done? With humor and enthusiasm? Are you apt to volunteer to help out? Do you tend to uplift every group you're in?

- **Hyperempathy:** Can you literally feel the feelings of others? Do you cry easily at movies, sad books, Hallmark television ads? Do you work in the healing professions?

- **Responsibility and resourcefulness:** Are you the go-to person in your family or at work? The one who holds the "tribal memory" of the place—the person who remembers where the old contracts are kept and what the minutes of the meeting from two years ago said? Do you often end up in leadership roles at work or at home?

- **Self-directed:** Are you a self-starter who works well without supervision? Are you highly motivated to learn new things, figure systems out, and solve problems?

- **Overachieving:** Have you ever been called an overachiever? Do you find that you usually work harder than others and have a hard time resting and taking care of yourself?

Psychologist Dr. George Simon, Jr., has also identified similar qualities that can become vulnerabilities in people at risk for manipulation:

- **Naïveté:** Do you simply believe that people can't possibly be as cunning, devious, and evil as your gut tells you they are? Do you assume that everyone is working toward the good of others?

- **Conscientiousness:** Are you harder on yourself than anyone else? Do you give the manipulator the benefit of the doubt when he hurts you? Are you too willing to blame yourself when the vampire goes on the attack?

- **Low self-esteem and low self-confidence:** Do you doubt that your needs and desires are legitimate? Do you have what it takes to face conflicts directly and effectively? Do you back down at the first sign of conflict and concede to the other? Are you easily manipulated by guilt and shame?

- **Intellectualization:** Do you always try to understand and explain the behavior of others rationally and logically? And make the mistake of believing that there must be a reason why the manipulator is acting like he is? Do you get so wrapped up in trying to understand others' points of view that you forget yourself? Do you have trouble accepting the fact that there are people in this world who fight too much and fight underhandedly just to get what they want?

Look at Yourself

Take a bit of time right now to think about the people in your life and your own character. Put on some soft music, light a candle, and let your mind wander. Go down the list and ask yourself if you can relate to any of the characteristics mentioned above. Answer the questions above as honestly as you can. And remember, many of these characteristics are laudable when it comes to being effective in your life in general. It's just that we don't understand how vampires can be so calculating and predatory. And so we are caught unawares.

Look at Others

Now that you've checked out your own likelihood for attracting vampires, look at your relationships and make a vampire list. Going back as far as you can remember, write out all the vampires you've encountered. If you're dealing with a vampire currently, chances are good that you've dealt with them throughout your life and that your first vampire was in your family—a parent or grandparent, a brother or sister, an aunt or uncle. Chances are also good that no one else in your family understood how power-fully manipulative these individuals were. Or how they adversely affected you.

Bring a past or present vampire to mind. Relive the moment when you first met them or started to work with them. If you were a child, did you get a stomach-ache when they came to the house? Do you remember trying to please them in order to protect yourself? Did they scare you or abuse you in some way? Did you end up giving them your power because nobody told you how to stand up to them?

It's very possible that your very first vampire was your mother or father. And that you were raised to be an "exten-sion" of them. Perhaps they were living their unlived hopes and dreams through you. Or that your entire life was devoted to making them look good.

As you go down your list of vampires, do you notice how similar they are? Go back to Chapter 5 and reread the characteristics of a vampire. Trust yourself in this exer-cise—especially if you start talking yourself out of what you know and what you feel.

Note that each time you can name a vampire and their tactics, you get closer and closer to dodging them in your day-to-day life. After a while, you'll be able to spot them before you've even had your first interaction with them. And even if they are so charming and clever that they get by your defenses, you'll begin to "wake up" sooner and sooner.

One of my colleagues puts it this way: "My mother had narcissistic tendencies and was very self-centered. I ended up 'marrying my mother.' That marriage lasted 23 years. Then I got myself into a relationship with a friend who was also a charming and charismatic female vampire.

I woke up after 12 years. Then there was a business associate with whom I tried to start a company. That ended after three years. At the same time, I began working with a charismatic women's empowerment teacher. I saw the light after five years—but we didn't have regular contact. Each time I'm able to spot the vampire tactics sooner and sooner. And each time I trust my gut and exit my pattern of over-giving to them, I congratulate myself. Sometimes I even notice the pattern the very first time I meet them and never get involved at all."

GIVE UP ON THE VAMPIRE

Once you've identified that someone is a vampire, there is only one move on the board. I've said it before and I'll say it again: You *must* assume that he/she will never change. You must get on with your own life and stop waiting for the day when that "potential" you see in them becomes a reality. The chances of this happening are basically nonexistent—and they won't change unless they are forced to by something as powerful as you giving up on them.

I will add this disclaimer. Sandra Brown and Dr. George Simon, both experts in this field of personality disorders, actually disagree about whether or not change is ever possible. Brown has never seen it in her 30 years of working with vampires and their victims. Simon, on the other hand, who has worked with these characters for 25 years, reports that he has occasionally seen someone change.

Remember that there is a spectrum of vampires here. Some individuals simply have narcissistic traits; others are full-blown psychopaths. Those on the milder end of the scale can sometimes change, but—as I mentioned above—they do so only when pressured by external circumstances like the loss of a relationship, status, money, or a job. They must know that they've been boxed into a corner. Their bad behavior has been identified and their tactics no longer work. Simon says that in settings of tough love, in which you keep calling the vampire on their behavior, some may change—but only if they feel enough shame and guilt (or threat of loss) to make them look in the mirror and actually want to change and be a better person.

In my entire career and life so far, I know of only one case where this has happened—and it helped save a marriage. This was not simply because the victim took the vampire back; it was because she was pretty much "out the door" and gave him an ultimatum. This was the key. She was no longer invested in the marriage or him— one way or another. She had reached that amazing stage known as *indifference*, and there is no narcissistic supply with indifference. The ball wasn't just not in her court; she had stepped off the court entirely, leaving him alone with the ball.

She told him that he had to move out for three months, and he had to work with a therapist who specialized in narcissistic personality disorder—meaning a therapist who couldn't be manipulated by his vampire tactics. Because he had a lot to lose, he stuck to the rules. He went to the therapist twice per week and his behavior changed. Luckily, he was low enough on the narcissist scale to have some conscience and desire to change. But again, I want to state: *This is very rare.*

These incredibly rare instances of change are marked by the energy vampire experiencing contrition. George Simon notes that this is completely different from regret or remorse, which energy vampires may well express—"I've told you I'm sorry a hundred times, what more do you want from me?"—without really changing their behavior. Contrition means to be broken into many pieces, so with genuine contrition, vampires know that the onus is on them to *prove* they have changed and done everything in their power to become a better person. The bottom line is this: If someone is truly contrite, you won't have to do a thing. *They* will be responsible for doing everything in their power to change. In other words, the empath doesn't have to find just the right therapist, the right group, the right anything. The ball is solidly in the vampire's court.

But as I said, this is extremely rare, so you must proceed on the assumption that your vampire will never change. Put yourself first, stop waiting for the miracle, and get on with your life. Period. End of story. You really have to be done. You can't believe for a single minute that change is possible. That is the only way. Because in the one in a million chance that they will change, it will only happen when you are really done. It's a huge paradox.

I hesitated to tell you of this one single case because I feared it would inspire you to push through the pain in hopes of a change, and then not do the real work of disengaging. That's not how this works. You must do what is necessary to save yourself. From there you can decide if you want to put any of your energy toward this person. The one and only sure move on the board that will help you is to assume that the vampire will never change. You must disconnect as soon and as fully as possible. Like my friend, you want to get to total indifference, which is tough for empaths. Only then will you be in a position to plug energy leaks, restore your health, and call back your power.

FOCUS ON YOU

This chapter is called "Put Yourself First" because basically everything I'm talking about is focused on doing just that. But that can be hard to do, so I want to address it directly. Which brings me to one of my favorite quotes from Abraham as channeled by Esther Hicks: "You can't get sick enough to help sick people get better. You cannot get poor enough to help poor people thrive." When we feel it's our job to hang in there and donate our life energy to a bottomless pit in an effort to make them feel better, the only one who ends up suffering is us. It's like the old saying: "When you dim your light to please others, the whole world gets darker." So take care of yourself. Trying to never need any attention, affection, or a listening ear does not heal anything. In fact, it puts you at risk. You should not spend your entire life helping others at your own expense.

You count! Your well-being is a necessary part of the whole. And your well-being influences the whole in a very positive way. If you are constantly sacrificing yourself for the good of others, then who is going to save you? Nobody. If you don't learn how to include yourself, you'll end up in a cycle of coming back and sacrificing your well-being in a misguided attempt to save others. I jokingly tell people that if they don't clean up their difficult relationship with their child, husband, mother, wife, etc., they will come back as identical twins the next time. Talk about karma. Okay—I'm oversimplifying here. Obviously the concept of karma is far more complicated than this. But you get the point.

It has been estimated that the odds of you being here on this planet as you at this particular time—when you take into account how many people are on the planet and how many gazillions of sperm never make it to an egg—are 1 in 400 trillion. Take that in. You were meant to be here. It is your job to celebrate your excellence and your unique gifts. It is your job to use your specific talents in service to the world—a world that absolutely must include our own well-being. So you need to put yourself first. Focus on you and your well-being first and foremost. The fulfillment you'll find from doing this will astound and heal you.

The only way to heal and become the force of love you were meant to be is to make sure you give yourself the benefit of the doubt. Treat yourself as well as you treat everyone else. Quench your own thirst first before sharing with others. Find the love inside. The kind that never fails you.

In order to shift your perspective on yourself, say this out loud every morning before you begin your day:

"I pledge allegiance to myself
and to my Soul for which I stand.
I honor my goodness, my gifts, and my talents.
I commit to remaining loyal to myself from
this moment forward for all of my days."

I call this a new Pledge of Allegiance. Mario Martinez calls doing something like this "accepting your greatness with humility." Whatever you call it, this act changes everything. If the pledge here doesn't work for you, make up your own. It's about acknowledging that you matter each and every day. The point is to say it over and over again until it gets into your subconscious. By using it daily, you'll soon start to consciously make choices that honor yourself. Then soon enough, you'll start making those choices without thinking about it. That's when the thought has become a hardwired belief.

Yes, putting yourself first can be hard—much harder said than done—but it's worth it. When you begin to do this, you will feel guilty—guaranteed. When that happens, you must notice the guilt and accept it. This alone takes away some of the power of guilt. I like to do a fun exercise whenever guilt pops up for me. As soon as I feel it, I fully and lovingly say to myself, "Nice going! You're nailing it! No one has ever done guilt better than you're doing it."

Believe it or not, completely accepting your guilt will help you release it much faster than hanging on to it and beating yourself up for it. It is when we resist feeling what we're really feeling that we get stuck. As the saying goes, "You've got to feel it to heal it." And though guilt and shame are incredibly painful feelings, they're far better felt and released than left smoldering inside. When you feel shame, guilt, sadness—or any other painful emotion—congratulate yourself!

CREATE BOUNDARIES

One of the most powerful tactics you can take to put yourself first is to create boundaries. Boundaries come in all shapes and sizes—from a complete cutoff to a managed minimization. Boundaries are absolutely key to your sanity, particularly if you suspect that your vampire has borderline personality disorder. Obviously, the best thing you can do to avoid being narcissistic supply is to completely cut off communication. End the marriage. Break up the relationship. Quit the job. But for many of us, this tactic won't work. You can't just walk out on your husband if you have children together. You can't just quit a job if you need money. And what if your vampire is one of your children? In any of these instances, the goal is to figure out how to minimize contact—or at least minimize being taken advantage of—as much as humanly possible.

Remember how I told you that at the beginning of my career the one negative review would haunt me, overtaking the joy that I should have felt from the 200 positive reviews? It would ruin my self-concept and mood for a couple of weeks. Well, I don't have to deal with that anymore because I set a boundary. I decided not to open the mail myself. I had a staff member do it—as a self-protection mechanism. And if the criticism were constructive, I'd make needed changes. But quite frankly, I don't remember more than a couple of instances over the years in which the criticism was constructive.

Now with social media, there is almost no way to avoid criticism and negativity—especially if you're putting yourself out there in any significant way. Of course the more of a public figure you are, the more negativity. I remember watching the 2017 Oscars, in which some of my favorite movie stars read the nasty tweets about themselves from that year right into the camera. It was stunning to see the wonderful Emma Stone read a tweet posted about her that stated, "Emma Stone always looks like a crack whore in every movie she's in." Ouch.

So the issue with this is to figure out a strategy to deal with negative reviews and criticism. As I was putting the finishing touches on this book, I did a Facebook Live presentation with a farmer friend of mine who grows antioxidant-rich black currants that I wanted my community to know about. Hundreds of people weighed in from all over the world, many contributing beautifully to the conversation. But there was one comment. A woman who said, "This would work a lot better if you just let him talk. You're taking over the conversation." Sting. There was the splinter again. Of course that was just her opinion. But it is the one thing I focused on for a while—given my lifelong pattern of trying to please and heal others—at the expense of myself.

Here's what I now do on social media—and you can figure out what will work in your situation. If someone is snarky or critical, I no longer try to "buff them up," send love, or try to explain my position. If the comment is nasty or a put-down, I just delete it. If it happens again, I simply press "ban user." My community Facebook page is my kingdom. And I am the Queen of my own Kingdom. Why would I let someone ruin it? I treat it like I treat my house. I wouldn't let anyone pollute it or leave trash lying around my yard, so why would I allow the digital equivalent? There are many opportunities for people to argue and be nasty on social media, but my page is *not* one of them.

There are so many situations in life where you can make a simple change to protect your energy. If there's someone at work you end up chatting with who sucks you dry every time you pass them on your way to the bathroom, find a different route to the bathroom. If there isn't a different route, is there a different bathroom?

Does your friend call only when he needs something? Don't answer—but don't make excuses. Behavior is everything. If he ever gets up the courage to ask you if you've been avoiding him, call him out on his behavior. Be prepared for this to not go over well.

One of my friends, whom I'll call Sandy, works at a company where the general manager is a bully (and a vampire). Sandy eventually became sick of the angry outbursts and insults that he had to endure from this guy. He finally said, "What have I ever done to you to make you treat me this way?" And that was the end of it. Sandy stood up to the bully and the bully went elsewhere. I recently heard that that same bully went a bit too far and was fired. There is also trouble in his marriage. Pretty standard for your average vampire.

The Power of No

One of the best ways to minimize your interaction with energy vampires is to become "empowered in the negative." In other words, learn how to turn people down, even if you have to hurt them a bit in the process. This is essential. Be like those old drug commercials: Just Say No.

I know what you're thinking, *If saying no were so easy, I would have already started doing it.* But here's the thing: Saying no just takes practice. It is possible to say no in a way that doesn't injure the person you're talking to. It's all about compassion, which you have in spades. If no doesn't come easily to you at first, then at least say, "I'll get back to you." The main thing you need to master is to stop the knee-jerk YES. Here's a good way to say no: "I'm so honored that you asked, but I simply must decline. I know you'll understand."

Here's a quick exercise that you can use as you start to practice your no. The next time someone asks you to do something, take a breath and tune in to how you are feeling. Does your stomach drop when you think of saying yes? Are you excited? Are you annoyed that they asked? By paying attention to these sensations, you'll know pretty quickly if you actually want to say yes. And if it's not a "hell yes," it's a no. If it's a no, always remember that if you say yes when you want to say no, your ambivalence will adversely affect the energy of the entire endeavor. You aren't doing anyone any favors with your yes.

Start out saying no on a small scale. *Do you want a soda? No. Is it okay for me to throw my coat on your bed? No. Please put it here instead. Is it okay if I eat while we talk? No.* Watch how a two-year-old does it. That is the age at which we naturally develop boundaries and learn the word *no*. My two-year-old granddaughter delights me when she doesn't like something I'm doing and says, "Lulu, stop it." Loud and clear.

Once you get a bit more comfortable saying no—or "I'll get back to you"—for the little things, you can move on to the big things. But don't just jump in. Imagine a big situation where you want to say no but haven't had the guts to in the past. Walk yourself through it. Step by step. You might even bring to mind a situation in which you said yes when you meant no. How did it turn out? Did you end up being pleased that you said yes? Or, as so often happens, did the situation just get worse and worse? There is no time in the unconscious. When you replay a situation or feeling as though it were happening in the present, it reinforces the situation. Neither the mind nor body knows the difference between the past and the present. They don't know if you are experiencing something in the present moment or in a memory. All they know is that you are experiencing an emotion associated with a situation. That's real enough for the brain to log this as a real experience. And when you do this—repeatedly— you grow neural pathways that determine how you will react in your life. So the goal in this visualization is to create a neural pathway that helps you say no. Go back into that same situation, and in your imagination, say "I simply can't." Practice saying it over and over again. Do this until it becomes so automatic that it will be the first thing you think of to say. And remember this, no excuse or explanation is necessary. Just say, "I simply can't." No discussion necessary. You don't owe them a thing.

Now go on to a different situation. Imagine a friend asking you to go out with them to do something. Imagine the sinking feeling in your gut. But the simultaneous feeling that you don't want to let them down or disappoint them.

And then figure out the exact words you would use to turn your friend down. Picture yourself saying those words and picture your friend's response. Walk through the fear. And then do it again. Replay this movie over and over until it doesn't elicit fear in you.

Once you face down your fears of saying no, you'll be much better able to stick to situations that don't drain you.

Broken Wing

Another tactic I love that is all about creating boundaries—or completely disengaging with an energy vampire—is called "broken wing." A while back, when I was just starting to learn about energy vampires, I was involved in business with a man who turned out to be one of the cleverest psychopaths I've yet run into. He was treating our business partnership quite unprofessionally. In fact, he was just love-bombing me. Telling me how special I was. How incredibly skilled and beautiful. How lucky any man would be to marry me. You get the picture. I wasn't particularly attracted to him, but at the time, getting all those love poems and gifts was kind of intoxicating. The thing was, he always played a kind of shell game with our relationship—always changing the contract between us. And I never could get a straight answer about our agreement. I needed a way to create some boundaries and get this man to stick with business.

At the same time I was in this business partnership, I was also consulting with a psychologist, who taught me a technique she had used for years in her practice—a technique that worked especially well with borderline personality disorder. You just feign illness or a family emergency. In other words, you turn the tables on them. Now *you* are the bird with the broken wing; you're the one who has the need, not them. When you do this, they evaporate like fog in the hot sun.

This also works with online dating—a place that is crawling with energy vampires. A common tactic vampires will use is that they will lead with a wound like "I'm a widower," "I'm recently divorced and my ex is keeping my kids from me," and so on. If this happens, you should get suspicious. Then trust your gut. If a part of you feels afraid in any way, pull the "broken wing" and watch how quickly they cut off all communication.

Milligrams of Love

Everything we've discussed about boundaries up until this point has been about avoiding minor situations in your life. So what about the major ones? How can you set up boundaries in a marriage that you can't walk away from? What about with your mother? Or your sister? This is where things get a bit more complicated.

Dr. Mario Martinez teaches that love is toxic to a toxic person. And that there are only so many milligrams of love that a toxic person can take before they become mean or nasty. You know when they've reached their maximum dosage when they start criticizing you or being negative. Here's an example. You go to visit your mother. You haven't seen her in a while and you're happy to see her, hoping that this time the visit will be more positive. And all goes well—for about 30 minutes. After that, she begins to criticize your hair, your career, your children. You get the picture. It is at this point that you make your exit. You absolutely must learn that you do not have the power to make her happy or uplift her once she goes negative. Instead, you must leave, or at the very least, close the door and go to another room. You can say, "I notice that you've started to be critical. So I'm leaving." Do not make the mistake of reacting emotionally. Don't cry, don't beg, don't expect to have your feelings validated. Just leave. It's that simple.

Now here's the part that you must master: You must learn to be okay with the fact that they won't like it when you create a healthy boundary. No vampire likes to be called on their tactics. You've seen the movies and read the books about vampires, right? They can't stand to be out in the sunlight. When you set a healthy boundary and stick with it, you're shining a light on the vampire. They'll retreat into the darkness. You must also learn to be okay with the fact that they will then criticize you and try to involve other family members—and try to get them to be against you. Do not make the mistake of thinking that you can defend yourself against this. You can't. Just walk away. Don't try to make your case. At the end of the day, you will be judged by your behavior—not your words. Walking away is very powerful.

Another tactic for keeping in touch with vampires without being drained too much includes doing some careful cultivation of activities that you can do together. Figure out what kinds of things work best with your vampire and what the ideal time frame should be. I have a friend whose father is a bona fide vampire. They share a mutual love of the theater, the arts, and museums, so she has learned that an afternoon or evening outing to a movie or the theater—with an early or late dinner—is ideal. They both enjoy themselves and she doesn't get sucked into his drama or into a futile attempt to make him happy. She learned long ago that spending the night at his house—with his current wife and their son—simply doesn't work. It always leaves her drained and tearful. Now she knows better.

The last piece of advice for creating boundaries with folks you have to interact with is simply to be as boring and devoid of energy as you can be. This is referred to as "gray rock." It works just the way it sounds: You act like a gray rock. Answer questions with "Yes" and "No." Limit contact as much as humanly possible. Remember, all vampires want is narcissistic supply, so gray-rocking them will turn off the faucet.

THE IN-BETWEEN

When you become skilled at identifying energy vampires and you start creating boundaries, you move into a place I call the in-between. This is the time between learning about vampires and cutting them off completely. During this time, you will likely feel lonely and sad for a number of reasons. The first is because, though you have stopped giving vampires your energy, you are not yet to the point where you will have attracted a welcoming new group of friends who are not vampires. When you are still in relationship with a vampire—even a relationship that is edging slowly toward zero—you are most likely going to be invisible or unappealing to people who can spot vampires a mile away. You're also not going to be available for a conscious, equal partnership with anyone. As one of my old-soul empath friends shared recently, "I used to be so nice and overaccommodating that I was virtually invisible to truly healthy people. If I'm honest, though, I probably wouldn't have been interested in them either since my self-esteem was totally dominated by how much I could help others solve their problems."

The other thing that adds to your loneliness and sadness is that you may find your inner circle of close friends dwindling to just a handful. Maybe even to just one or two. I often joke that after I ditched "frenemies" and other aspects of Darkness, I could count the number of friends I interacted with regularly on half of one hand.

The final reason you may feel sad in the in-between is because you're going to start to feel some things that you likely haven't felt for years—maybe since early childhood, when you likely started to please energy vampires as a way to fit in and be accepted in your family or group. Throughout the years, you have worked to push down painful emotions that came from being shamed, abandoned, or betrayed by your family and friends. Once you shift the focus to you, these emotions will arise, and you will sometimes feel overwhelmed by them.

So here's what you have to do. You have to feel how sad you are. But please remember not to beat yourself up about it. You are down to the bedrock of that wounded little kid, and she needs more love, not less. Imagine a precious two-year-old and treat yourself with the same kindness and gentleness.

Please also realize that as you devote your time and energy to taking the necessary steps to protect and empower yourself, you are making an amazing shift. Your hard work *will* pay off, and soon enough a whole new group of healthy supportive people will enter your life. So don't fret too much about the in-between. It'll pass. You just need to keep focusing on healing yourself.

Chapter 7

HEAL YOUR
VAMPIRE TRAUMA

Now that you've (hopefully) put a bit of distance between you and the energy vampire who's been draining you, it's time to start healing because, no, just leaving a relationship that's draining you won't make everything okay.

In fact, most people who get out of these relationships experience a great deal of grief and remorse. They wonder, *How in the world have I allowed myself to be duped for so long?* This is normal. Just remember, very few people have understood the dynamics at play in vampire-empath relationships until fairly recently. Even in the popular musical *Carousel* the main character waxes poetic about her love for the carnival barker who just hit her! Our entire culture has enabled these characters for centuries, so don't beat yourself up. The goal now is to move forward. To heal.

You must learn to face the void—the emptiness inside that you've been filling up with trying to save the vampire and provide them with your love, attention, etc. You must be willing to be with your emotions and grief long enough to heal them. If you don't address these emotions you're likely to get into another relationship that will harm you just as much. So let's get started.

TRUSTING YOURSELF

One of the first things you have to start doing is to learn how to trust yourself again. Years of being lied to, manipulated, shamed, and made to feel crazy can really take a toll on this ability and your ability to simply think clearly.

The work of Sandra Brown has demonstrated that many women who've been in relationships with vampires actually develop what is called cognitive dissonance. Having had the wool pulled over their eyes for years, they can't think straight. Literally. Skilled vampires always make themselves look like the victim. And we end up seeming like the bad guy. My friend Carol, who has a Ph.D. and recently ended a nearly two-decade-long marriage to an energy vampire, used to text me or send me voice memos when she felt crazy. She'd tell me the situation and what was going on. Because her husband had created such self-doubt for so many years and had used his tactics to confuse her, she needed to know that she wasn't crazy. Every time she'd call, I could tell her what the tactic was he was using. But mostly I reassured her that she wasn't crazy. And that her gut perceptions about the situation were right on the mark.

Many people in these relationships, however, don't have a "reality check" on their side. Often so much of their focus is on the vampire that they don't call in the people who can help them stay grounded. Obviously, people can recover from this, but it takes work. When you've been subjected to manipulative tactics of an energy vampire for years, you begin to doubt what you know.

There are many ways to build trust in yourself, but some of the ones that I've found most effective are:

Educate yourself: Though vampires have been around for centuries—manipulating families, towns, companies, and even entire countries—it is only in the past 25 years or so that the field of mental health has been able to diagnose these individuals and name how they operate. The more you educate yourself about vampires, in particular narcissistic personality disorder, the more clearly you will be able to recognize it. This will help you immensely in your recovery because learning about this topic is incredibly validating; it makes you see that your perceptions of the person were correct and that the issue isn't with you.

The internet is full of great information about character-disordered people and how they operate. Melanie Tonia Evans has a regular YouTube channel known as ThriverTV. George Simon, Ph.D., has many good interviews on YouTube as well. Google "narcissistic personality disorder" or "narcissistic abuse" and you will be amazed at the richness of online resources you will find. Read and watch a variety of different people discussing these issues. Again, this is all about validation, which will help you build trust in yourself. A nice bonus of this education is that you'll also get a lot of tips about other ways to heal.

Find a reality check: Just as Carol had me as a reality check during her marriage (and still does today), you need someone clearheaded and trustworthy whom you can contact when you're feeling uncertain about a situation. It's very important that you have at least one other person who can see the situation clearly. Often this will be a good friend who knows you well and who has not been taken in by your vampire.

Work with your gut: One of the perks of being an empath is that we are in fact highly intuitive. Our guts tell us what is really going on in most situations, but over the years of being with an energy vampire, we've lost the ability to believe what we feel. But if our very first reaction to someone or some situation is anger, for example, we need to trust that. Remember that anger is simply a sign that a need isn't being fulfilled. As you begin to heal, you can do some work to prove to yourself how accurate these feelings actually are. Start paying attention to what your gut says, and then follow that feeling. But not just that. Keep track of whether the person or situation you chose to avoid (or become close with) plays out in the way you expected. Write these things down. Keep a gut instincts journal. Soon enough, you'll see that your gut is a pretty great indicator of the true energy of every situation.

Pat yourself on the back—regularly: Whenever you catch yourself doing something right, pat yourself on the back: "I fold laundry so beautifully. I love the way it looks when I'm finished. [Pat on the back.]" Or perhaps, "Today I spent 15 minutes meditating. I love that I took the time to do this for myself. [Pat on the back.]" "I smiled at a stranger today on the subway—and we had a moment of true human connection: I loved it. [Pat on the back.]" "I chewed my food beautifully today and just loved the taste. I'm an amazing self-nurturer. [Pat on the back.]"

This pat can be real or imagined; the important thing here is that you are recognizing the good in you and reinforcing your self-worth.

The process of learning to trust yourself again isn't a quick turnaround. You likely had years of someone taking this away, and you can't expect it to just come back. So give yourself plenty of time and support as you reclaim your ability to think clearly.

LET THE VAMPIRE GO ENTIRELY

I know this may be hard to hear since you are so prone to caring for people, but you need to stop worrying about the well-being of the vampire. While you may have created physical boundaries—not seeing the vampire, not taking calls, not interacting, and so on—you also need emotional boundaries. I can hear you now. "What about so-and-so? He's human too, you know? If one out of five people is a vampire, who in the world will care for him?" I've got news for you, sweetheart—vampires will always manage to get the care they need. Count on it. I have never, ever seen a single vampire "go without." They remarry in record time. Or find someone to take care of them. The only one who gets hurt in this process is someone like you. So just stop giving the vampire your life's blood. Got it? And remember this—if you're reading this book, it means that the life lesson in self-worth and self-care that you have needed to learn by having your life's blood sucked by a vampire is now over. There will, unfortunately, be hundreds of people who have not learned that lesson—who honestly aren't ready for it. They will continue to take care of the vampires.

GET SUPPORT

When we finally "get it" about vampires and are in early recovery, we desperately need support—and not just from our "reality check" friend. The help of a psychotherapist who specializes in narcissistic abuse recovery can be invaluable in these situations. Sadly, because the field of mental health and psychotherapy hasn't recognized energy vampires until the past 25 years or so, a huge amount of damage has been done to those seeking help from traditional therapists who don't understand the vampire dynamic. Dr. George Simon, Jr., wrote the first edition of *In Sheep's Clothing* in 1996. Back in those days, almost no one in the field of mental health understood character disorders. He has been doing workshops and teaching therapists for more than 25 years, but when he started, therapists often walked out of the room as he was teaching. They simply didn't believe what he was saying. It flew in the face of their training and their beliefs.

Though the light is dawning, there are still far too many therapists and mental health professionals who don't understand how narcissist-empath relationships work and what is needed to heal from them. If you couldn't create a complete split from your vampire relationship and have decided to do couple's therapy, finding a therapist who knows how to deal with character-disordered individuals is even more important. If they don't, they may succumb to the manipulative tactics of the vampire and actually hurt your recovery. I've heard too many stories about women being shamed in therapy because the therapist was taken in by charming, silver-tongued narcissists. This is why it's absolutely critical that you get the right kind of help. Therapy is useless at best, and harmful at worst unless the therapist knows exactly how to deal with character disorders, which includes naming and confronting their behavior as a first step.

To find a therapist who specializes in healing from having a relationship with an energy vampire, look for someone who understands character disorders. Ask them, point blank, what they know about narcissistic personality disorder or borderline personality disorder. If they are taken aback by your question, find someone else.

Sandra Brown began her work with psychopaths about 25 years ago and has done ongoing research on the types of women who are attracted to them. She offers excellent retreats for women who are recovering from narcissistic abuse. I've included information about these—and a number of other resources for recovery—in the Resources section at the back of this book (page 201).

In addition to the help of a therapist it is essential to find others who have been where you are. In general, the culture doesn't understand narcissistic abuse. That's why the retreats Sandra holds are so great—you get to heal with others who are healing from similar situations. However, if you can't make it to one of these retreats, you can certainly join an online group. Melanie Tonia Evans runs an online program for narcissistic abuse recovery that includes a private Facebook group. People from all over the world have found help here. Again, check out the resources on page 201 for more information.

Be careful about any group you join. You don't want to join a group where the members are simply complaining—a group in which the "support" comes solely in the form of consoling and reinforcing the victimhood of people. In groups like this, people don't make progress. They get mired in the pain of the relationship. Or taking the inventory of the vampire. Over and over and over. What you're looking for is freedom, health, and joy. You want out of spinning in the drama of the vampire-empath dance, and you'll never remember who you really are if you keep identifying as a victim who has no power.

If you can't find a narcissistic abuse recovery group that you are comfortable with, you can try Al-Anon or CoDA (Co-Dependents Anonymous). Though Al-Anon is specifically for individuals who are in a relationship with an alcoholic, the dynamic of living with an alcoholic is similar to that of living with a vampire. They have behavior that you wish you could change, but can't. But you're overly focused on changing them so that you can feel better about yourself. Bottom line: You are powerless over their behavior. (That is the basis of the first step of the 12-step program: "We admitted we were powerless over . . . fill in the blank.") CoDA is for people who have experienced compulsive codependency in their relationships and are trying to heal and create healthy relationships. Sandra Brown rightfully points out that women with super traits are decidedly not codependent, nor are they relationship addicts. Their light and goodness and super traits are just misunderstood. And so these women (and men) are constantly mislabeled and misdiagnosed. And until now, they have not been widely accepted for the super humans they can be. Hence you may find that 12-step meetings just don't quite "hit the nail on the head." People with super traits are literally "blind" to a vampire's darkness. Still, these meetings can be helpful. The quality of them varies, so you may have to try out a number of different groups to find an Al-Anon or CoDA group you love. Just remember, it's not about the alcoholic or the vampire. It's about you. The reason 12-step programs can be so helpful is that, very often, empaths become addicted to their vampire partners. You are dealing with many of the same problems as the people who attend these meetings. Another benefit: These meetings are free, and they're held all over the world.

CLEARING OLD ENERGY

Another important piece of getting past the trauma of a vampire relationship is to focus on clearing old, stuck energy that comes from unexpressed emotions. We empaths often feel most comfortable engaging in "love and light" types of activities, such as prematurely attempting to forgive and send love to the vampires in our lives. But you must not do this. It will delay your healing. You must first feel as bad as you're feeling and move your emotions of anger and hurt out of your body. You do this by feeling them fully and expressing them in a safe way.

One of my radio show callers was one month away from finalizing her divorce to a vampire who was leaving her penniless. He was a very successful CEO and a "pillar of the community" who, she said, specialized in covert manipulation. She finally, after nearly 20 years of marriage, got up the courage to divorce him. She called in to tell me how helpful my show with Dr. George Simon had been. She then went on to tell me that she was working with a spiritual healer whom she really loved. Unfortunately, she still suffered from esophageal spasms regularly—a gastrointestinal disorder that had begun several years before as she had started to wake up to the character of her spouse. She often felt a pit in her stomach at other times as well, though the esophageal spasms were a bit different. Though she had had minimal contact with her vampire, I knew that he still had his "hooks" in her. So I took her through an imprint removal process—which I will teach you below—that I learned from the late Peter Calhoun, a former Episcopal priest turned shaman. Part of that process involves identifying where in your body you feel the stuck energy and then imagining that the vampire is sitting right in front of you so you can share your true emotions with him. As I led her through this, I told her to let him have it and encouraged her to say out loud (for medicinal purposes), "Jerry—you f**king bastard. I forgive you for all the pain and suffering you have caused me. And I send you on your path of healing." The expletive was absolutely necessary to move the stuck energy from her body. And the feeling in the pit of her stomach went away after that. And I have no doubt that her esophageal spasms are well on their way to healing as well.

Imprint Removal Process

The late Peter Calhoun developed this process to assist people in removing adverse energy imprints in their bodies. I have found that this process is invaluable in getting to the root of the problem and clearing it. It is best done with two people. Let's call one the healer and the other the subject.

1. The subject—whose imprint is being removed—sits in a chair that has room around it for the healer to move.

2. The healer asks the subject to identify where in the body he/she is feeling the stuck energy. It's usually in the throat, the heart, or the solar plexus.

3. The healer now "preps" the healing field as follows.

    He says, "With Archangel Michael's cobalt blue sword of light, I now cut all energy cords to [name of subject]." Then the healer literally imagines cutting energy cords around the body of the subject with a sword. If the healer is intuitive or can sense energy, she or he may well see or sense swords, knives, ropes, or other objects that need to be energetically cut or removed from the subject's body. Go ahead and cut them or remove them. Just the intent to do so will usually do the trick. But it's fun to play around with Archangel Michael's sword.

Now the "field" is clear, and the subject is ready for the imprint removal.

4. The subject imagines her vampire sitting in front of her and feels the feeling in their body that is associated with the vampire. (By the way, the vampire can be someone from the past and even someone who has died. The imprint remains until it is cleared.)

5. Now the healer encourages the subject to tell the vampire exactly how she feels. Here are the words you use: "[Fill in the vampire's name] . . . I forgive you for [fill in the blank], and I send you on your path of healing."

The stronger the language and emotion that are expressed, the faster the imprint will be removed. Example: "Mabel, you wretched bitch, I forgive you for sleeping with my best friend and completely betraying my trust, and I send you on your path of healing." Or "Sam, I forgive you for leaving me for another woman. And abandoning me with no support for our children. You are such an asshole, and I send you on your path of healing." Keep going along these lines as long as the energy is strong. Usually a couple of strong sentences are all that is needed.

The subject doesn't go on and on and on. This is not a therapy session. It's designed to move energy out of the body.

In imprint removals you want to let the vampire have it. As strongly as possible. In no uncertain terms. Being "nice" or "politically correct" will not get the job done.

You can tell when the subject has identified the imprint in their body, when they start to feel really emotional—either tearful or angry. Remember, the phrase is "Gail (or whoever), I forgive you for [fill in the blank], and I send you on your path of healing." You no longer want to hang on to this energy. This is IT.

After the subject has let the vampire have it—and sent them on their path of healing—the next phrase is:

"And I forgive myself for [fill in the blank]." For example: "I forgive myself for staying with you for so long when I knew in my heart I should have left much sooner."

Generally, it is in the self-forgiveness that the subject is owning her/his part of the interaction. And this is very often where the biggest healing and removal takes place.

Now the healer says to the subject: "Are you ready to transmute this pattern in the violet flame?"

If the subject feels complete with what needed to be said, they will say YES.

At this point, the healer reminds the subject to say, "I now transmute this pattern in the violet flame."

The healer imagines that the subject is sitting in a violet flame, which is consuming all the old energy.

The healer asks the subject to let them know when the feeling they had (pressure in the chest, lump in the throat, etc.) has gone. That is how you know that the imprint has been removed. Sometimes it will take more than one try. (Note: the violet flame is a nonphysical healing energy available to all humans. If you want more information, google "violet flame." You'll be amazed by how much you can learn.)

When the imprint has been burned away, you now need to "pack" the areas of removal to seal them. You do this with midnight blue and golden light. So the healer literally says, "I am now packing the areas of removal with midnight blue and golden light." Literally imagine using your hands to pack the areas of energy release with this light.

Encourage the subject to rest. This is real psychic surgery. And it's powerful. It's important to rest afterward. I've had many people simply have to take a nap for several hours after an imprint removal. So prepare for this. And don't do the removal until the subject will be able to rest afterward.

One more thing: Very often, the removal of one imprint will bring up another, deeper one. If that happens, don't suffer in silence. It's very important to do an imprint removal on the next layer as soon as possible. That's how we heal—in layers!

Chapter 8

A DEEPER HEALING JOURNEY

Healing the direct effects of your relationship with a vampire is an important part of your progress; however, you must also address the deeper wounds—the ones you bear from childhood—because these are the things that made you vulnerable to a vampire in the first place. So now it's time for a deeper emotional healing, which is also the first step in deep physical healing.

FINDING SELF-LOVE AND SELF-WORTH

Most people coming out of narcissistic abuse have to do some work on their egos. While energy vampires have a superior ego—they believe they're better than everybody else and that the world is there to serve them—empaths have what spiritual teacher Matt Kahn calls an "inferior" ego. The inferior ego has to doubt itself to stay alive. This problem is the exact opposite of what we generally think of as an ego trip, but it's an ego trip nonetheless. Inferior egos get fed by beating ourselves up for our shortcomings and looking for things that need to be improved. As you know, we empaths have had childhoods that take us down the path of inferiority—and for old-soul empaths, this path started in other lifetimes, meaning we are often born feeling unworthy. In the youth of any empath, needs and emotions get neglected. We feel the energy blockages in our parents' hearts and the hearts of those around us. This feels awful. And as Matt Kahn says, we make the decision that "In order to be liked by them, I have to be like them." And so we lower our vibration to match their level. Doing anything else feels too awful.

In a narcissistic relationship, our inferior ego gets fed all the time, which is one of the reasons we stay. Our ego's constant need to prove our worthiness so we can finally "measure up" is the perfect foil for the narcissist to keep us striving for a target we can never reach, because they keep moving the goalpost. It won't matter if we finally weigh the right amount, look a certain way, earn enough money to make the narcissist happy. We will never be "enough" in their eyes or our own.

One my patients, who divorced her handsome lawyer vampire after she discovered he was having an affair, admitted that she used to look at him and say, "But I'm doing better, aren't I?" She was referring to her weight and body image—and looking to him to validate her, which no vampire is ever going to do. Another of my patients told me that at the funeral of her father-in-law, her own vampire husband (whom she has since divorced) introduced her as his "million-dollar baby" because she was working her ass off to pay all the bills and keep him happy by sending him on fancy adventure trips. She thought it would help with his "depression."

But I digress—to make a point: To protect ourselves from this vulnerability, we must work to reverse our inferior egos. We must not feed them. But this cannot be done with our minds. They can only be reversed with our hearts. We need to wake up from the illusion of unworthiness, an illusion that has undoubtedly been fed and watered for centuries.

In order to heal your heart and shed the illusion that you're not worthy, you need to tap into your emotions. In his book *How to Be an Adult in Relationships: The Five Keys to Mindful Loving*, David Richo beautifully puts forth the qualities that every relationship needs to be strong and fulfilling. He calls these things the five A's: attention, appreciation, approval, affection, and allowing. If you are in a relationship with a person who provides you with these things, you will experience the healing benefits of true intimacy. You'll feel seen, valued, cared for, and worthy. These five A's will feed a healthy sense of self and ego—and help take away that feeling of worthlessness. Luckily, you don't have to wait for someone else to provide these for you. The most important relationship in your life is the one you have with yourself. So start there. Healer and women's health expert Tami Lynn Kent added mantras to each of the five A's to make them even more powerful:

- Attention: I see you

- Appreciation: I value you

- Approval: I accept you

- Affection: I love you

- Allowing: I trust you

I suggest that you say these each morning out loud to yourself while looking right into your eyes in the mirror. You'll feel an energy shift by day 20—or even earlier. And in the future, you can judge the value of your relationships by whether or not these five A's are present or absent.

It's all a part of learning how to love yourself more and reversing that inferior ego. In a radio show interview I did with Dr. George Simon, we took a call from a woman who had left a relationship with an energy vampire and had had no contact with him for a year. But she said she was still struggling with self-love. Dr. Simon asked her how often she was supporting herself—how often she was giving herself appreciation, approval, and affection when she did something right. Turns out it had been a very long time. Dr. Simon noted that people who grow up with a narcissistic parent (and who, therefore, are often attracted to vampires later on) don't know what it's like to feel the support of an arm around their shoulder telling them that they are valued and loved. The medicine that heals this—other than a reparative relationship with a therapist, spouse, or good friend is self-approval.

RESPECT YOUR SHADOW

Reversing the inferior ego trip is a great place to start for healing our feelings of unworthiness, but there is likely a lot more work that needs to be done. We must also learn to respect our shadow—that part of us we try to hide so others won't know how we "really" are. This includes our negativity, sorrow, jealousy, anger, and grief. These will never go away until they have been acknowledged. And respected.

Matt Kahn tells a very funny story in one of his You-Tube videos about how he was doing his "I love you" practice—just saying "I love you" out loud to himself—and a voice in his head reared up and said, "Go f**k yourself." Clear as day. From that Matt learned about the potency of the shadow. It's the part of us that got rejected, blamed, and ignored—even when, as little children, we were coming from love. It's the part of us that says, "Well—that love bullshit never worked. So there. I'm certainly not going to try that crap again." It's that little wounded child who lives inside each and every one of us. This child can simply be part of you or it can rule your life.

The way to respect your shadow is to tell that little kid inside, "I'm so sorry, sweetie. I'm so sorry that happened to you." And mean it. The fastest way to the Divine inside is through taking care of the wounded child inside—who will keep bugging you until you stop neglecting him or her. In fact, that little wounded child will run your endocrine, immune, and central nervous systems until you take the time to meet her needs and stop neglecting her.

Part of respecting your shadow and caring for your inner child actually involves something I talked about before: praising yourself when you mess up. Whenever you do something that you consider a mistake—like spilling something, tripping, forgetting an appointment, feeling sad, getting angry, or feeling stuck—notice it and congratulate yourself. This is so counterintuitive that it will instantly shift your energy. Here's an example: You just spilled something on the table. You say to yourself, "Wow—I really did an amazing job spilling that milk. It takes a genius to make a mess this big from one tiny move of my hand." Or maybe you wake up feeling sad about being lonely. You say to yourself, "I'm feeling so sad and lonely. I am NAILING IT. No one has ever done sad and lonely as well as I'm doing it."

Get the picture? You'll actually make yourself laugh. And your shadow will eventually recede and stop running your life. Why? Because you have respected and acknowledged it. And you've cared for that wounded kid inside who never got the attention she needed.

As long as your inner child is grief-stricken, angry, lonely, or feeling unlovable, your outer experience in the world is going to re-create your wounds. And as long as that unhealed child is at the control panel of your life, you'll be nothing but a smorgasbord for vampires.

In her book *Repetition: Past Lives, Life, and Rebirth*, clinical psychologist Dr. Doris E. Cohen teaches that we keep repeating patterns from our childhood until we've brought love and understanding to that child. Here's a fast-track way to do that I learned from Doris. It's called the Seven Steps of Rebirth. And you can use it whenever you feel triggered by an outer event or are feeling discomfort of any kind.

- Step 1: STOP

    While saying "stop," visualize a stop sign.

- Step 2: Breathe

    Breathe in deeply through your nose. Remember to keep your arms and legs uncrossed, feet on the floor. Hold the breath for a count of four. Exhale a bit longer than the inhale for a count of five. Keep your facial muscles relaxed.

- Step 3: Acknowledge "Whoops. There I go again."

    Affirm that you're the author of your story. "Whoops, there I go again" will help you acknowledge your story without judgment.

- Step 4: Get a number

    Allow the first number that enters your mind to come into awareness. This is going to be the age of the child whom the adult is meeting in the next step.

- Step 5: Meet the child

    Create a magical nature scene—a magical garden—where you meet your child self, giving him or her love and reassurance, remembering to call on the Loving Angels of the Light. See what the child is doing. See if he or she will come and sit on your lap or give you a hug.

- Step 6: Separate from the child

    Reassure the child that she is safe, sound, and loved. Then detach yourself, leaving him or her in the safety of the garden with the angels.

- Step 7: Return to the present as an adult

    State your name, the date, and your location in order to ground yourself back in present time as your adult self, feeling alert, refreshed, revived, and replenished.

Take your time going through the steps. Each of them is precise. Don't skip steps. They are designed to create profound healing through the process of meeting your inner child, separating from him/her, and then returning to the present as an adult.

Remember that you MUST disconnect from your inner child each time you visit or else you stay connected to the wounded energy.

Over the ensuing 40 days, you will notice how she changes. She becomes happier. If you skip one day, you have to go back and start the 40 days all over again. This builds your intent and also adds immeasurably to the power of this practice.

I have done this exercise repeatedly over the years. After the initial 40 days, you can do shorter periods of time for specific issues. For example, after getting in touch with some unresolved pain from when I was 12, I visited my 12-year-old self in the magic garden for 13 days.

On another occasion, about five years or so after my divorce, I went into the magic garden and met, healed, and separated from my former married self and the shock of the divorce, which, at the time, felt like someone had put a knife in my heart *and* shot me. When I had a session with Doris about that, she told me that, energetically, the bullet was still there and the knife wound had to be stitched up. I visualized all of that day by day while I did the exercise. As a surgeon, I found that I knew exactly how to care for my own bleeding heart. By the 40th day, the "patient" (my former self) was jumping for joy. But many times during the 40 days, she was just sleeping soundly. Almost in a coma!

I introduced this technique to a caller on my radio show who had been married for 40 years. She was increasingly aware that her marriage was nonsupportive, but the reason for her call was to get some advice about painful sciatica down her left leg, which had just started about a month before. She told me that she had grown up on a farm and was the only girl. With five brothers. When she was seven, one of her brothers—who was only a year older than she—had held her left leg while another boy raped her. In addition to that, her only "friend" was a little dog who was precious to her. At one point, also when she was seven, the dog disappeared and she found out that it had gotten its legs cut off in a field mower. So she lost her only friend. Together we went through the magic garden exercise so that she could go back and attend to the needs of her inner seven-year-old. When I asked her if she could coax that little girl into her lap, she burst into tears and said, "I'm not sure I can get her to trust me."

This kind of situation is very common. When we are deeply wounded in childhood, a part of us no longer trusts. And it gets cut off from our consciousness. Nevertheless, this unconscious part of us is very powerful. And it will unduly influence our lives until we give it the attention, respect, and love it deserves. But not to worry. Over time—usually every day for 40 days—this inner child will begin to trust you. And each trip to the magic garden will become more and more fulfilling and healed.

In this case, my caller will go back to the magic garden day after day—each day coaxing her inner seven-year-old to come to her so she can love her. And each day, separating from her and coming back into the present. Within 40 days of consistent attention, the adult will have convinced the little girl that she is now safe and loved. And that the adult part has the skills and means to take over the wheel now. The child part can surrender and trust. Finally. And her outer life will reflect this shift.

HEALING OLD WOUNDS

In addition to respecting your shadow, you have to see and heal the wounds of your past, because these are actually what creates that shadow in the first place.

As empaths, we learned early on that we couldn't be our true selves. Throughout our lives—because we didn't understand our empathic nature—we became lint rollers for the unfelt pain of others. We took on stuff that wasn't our responsibility. And we did everything in our power to uplift others and make them feel better so that we could finally feel better too. We've twisted ourselves into pretzels to fit in and to avoid the three archetypal wounds that Mario Martinez discussed: shame, abandonment, and betrayal. Anxiety, painful sensitivity, and even addictions come from denying the truth of who we are in order to feel loved and safe.

Luckily we have a wonderful tool to help us figure out what needs to be healed in our lives. People and situations that trigger us on the outside, e.g., eliciting guilt and confusion, show us what has to happen on the inside so that we're not so vulnerable to our internalized wounds. For example, my friend Alice called me because she suspected that she had an energy vampire working for her in her health-care practice. This person was angry that Alice wasn't letting her do the teaching workshops that are part of the business, despite the fact that she was very new on the job and that Alice owned the business. She accused Alice of being "controlling." In the past, Alice would have taken this criticism to heart and started doubting herself and her competence. Asking herself, "Oh dear. Is that really true? Am I being controlling?"

Except now Alice had been through this same thing— an employee taking over and being disrespectful—several times. And she realized that she had nothing to be ashamed of or concerned about. In fact, as an empath, she saw that she had been feeling the shame that her employee *should* have been feeling but wasn't. I mean, really. What kind of person comes into a new employment situation and begins to find fault with everything and everybody, acting superior and thinking they know better than their boss? Who starts to undermine an enterprise from the very beginning? A vampire, that's who. Any astute psychiatrist or psychiatric nurse will tell you that you can always tell when there is a borderline on the psych ward. (And many of them are very clever and very high-functioning.) The staff starts fighting among themselves. That's how this particular type of vampire gets fed. Alice, a skilled healer, had finally seen this pattern one too many times in her own practice and with the kind of staff she kept attracting in her business. As her self-esteem and awareness of how vampires work began to improve, she recognized how she had been duped by these tactics. And how her inferior ego has bought into them. No longer. So now, instead of feeling bad, her response was, "Yes. This is my business and my material. You bet I like to control how it's presented to our clients." Game over.

Notice when you start to feel unsure of yourself and in what situations. When does self-doubt arise? What kind of criticism stays with you and ruins your day—no matter what you do to try to talk yourself out of it? What type of person elicits this in you? Your daily life will offer you an endless stream of information about what needs to be healed. For example, for many years I tried to hide my real beliefs about health, wellness, and spirituality from my more mainstream colleagues—always trying to fit in. I've even been set up on a few dates with men I respected but didn't know. And when they'd tell me they were going to check out my website before meeting me in person, I'd get nervous—figuring that they'd probably cancel the date after they realized what I was really all about. Not only did this not happen, these men were impressed and supportive. Shocker. The issue was all mine. And it's pretty much resolved at this point. But that took a while. Like so many empaths, I had become very adept at hiding my true self and trying to improve myself through self-discipline, hard work, and mastery. Complete with footnotes to prove what I knew. Now I rarely attract the kinds of vampires who were business as usual for so much of my life. And I'm instantly in touch with any anger I might feel when I'm expected to give with nothing in return.

We each need to learn how to make a connection to our unhealed—and often unconscious—wounds of abandonment, betrayal, lack of self-love, guilt, and shame. These are the wounds that attract vampires—like blood attracts sharks. But make no mistake, vampires also feed off our super traits: our endless goodwill and generosity.

Once you've learned how to see your wounds, you need to take steps to heal them, just as Alice had. Dr. Mario Martinez notes that for each of the archetypal wounds—abandonment, betrayal, and shame—there is a corresponding healing field that will ameliorate our suffering. These healing fields are energies that oppose the energy of the wound. They also turn out to be the character traits that we empaths have in spades. We simply have to acknowledge them within ourselves, instead of waiting for our tribes to change. The minute we feel and name the wound, and then simultaneously bring in the healing field, we begin to heal.

Let's start with abandonment. The healing field for abandonment is commitment. How many times have you remained in a bad situation—possibly long after everyone else has left? If you're a healer, or a parent, how many sleepless nights have you stood over a sick pet or sick child holding vigil? Sending prayers. Being a force for good. You have never abandoned your post. Celebrate yourself for that. And remember to keep these memories of commitment fresh in your mind and revisit them if you are ever besieged by feelings of abandonment. Your commitment to yourself and your own evolution is more than enough.

Next, the healing field for betrayal is loyalty. How many times have you personally stood up for a friend who might have been the victim of an energy vampire? Or come to the aid of a family member who needed you? Plenty, right? Let that stellar character trait sink in. Celebrate it and remember it if you ever feel betrayed. And never, ever betray yourself again.

Finally, let's look at shame. When you feel ashamed—and begin beating yourself up for your real or imagined shortcomings—the first thing you want to do is hide. You don't want anyone to know. You try to be perfect so that no one will find out that you're not perfect. Nothing is more painful than shame.

The healing field for shame is honor. The moment you feel shame, immediately think of something you did that was honorable. And while remembering honor helps shift the energy of shame, actually taking an honorable action in the moment can be extra powerful. Even small moments of honor are great. Perhaps helping a new mother with her baby at the airport, or taking a meal to a friend who just got home from the hospital. When you do this, feel the honor of that act, and then share it with a trusted friend who can celebrate you and reflect that honor back to you. You are indeed a good person. Remembering what is honorable about you and talking about it or, at the very least, feeling it, will lift the shame.

The other healing element for shame is light and humor. Shame simply can't last in these situations. So if you want to get rid of shame, you must talk about it—and not just the honorable things you do to shift it. You have to talk about the shame itself. Find a good friend. Find a therapist. Find a journal. Whatever you need to do to expose your shame to the light is a good first step. Then you have to turn it on its head. Almost all good comedy comes from doing this.

What do I mean by turning shame on its head? I mean, look at it and embrace it. For example, after my divorce I felt ashamed for not being able to make my marriage work. I blamed myself. I also felt as though I had ruined my daughters' lives. Moreover, I had also welcomed two cats from the local shelter into my home. I had become, almost overnight, the proverbial single, middle-aged woman with cats. As I felt my pain and humiliation and talked about it, I began to respect, embrace, and love myself for those feelings. Part of that was about experiencing how universal these feelings were for so many other people. Another part was that I began to realize that society tries to pigeonhole us through stereotypes. Yes, I was indeed a single, middle-aged woman with cats, but I was so much more than that. Soon after I began to talk about this shame, I completely reinvented myself and started to proclaim—proudly and with glee from up on the stage—that I was a "single, middle-aged woman with cats!"

One of the biggest obstacles faced by empaths is the fact that we have too often internalized the shame, abandonment, and betrayal from those around us. Too often we keep beating ourselves up, betraying ourselves, and abandoning ourselves. And we continue this until we see the pattern and remember how honorable, committed, and loyal we really are. We must learn how to unload this internalized shame, betrayal, and abandonment. And see it for the lie it really is.

It's never too late to start giving yourself and your needs the benefit of the doubt. It's time to commit to being there for yourself, your dreams, and the dictates of your soul. From this moment forward.

HEALING YOUR ANCESTRAL WOUNDS

Remember in Chapter 2, we discussed the fact that trauma experienced by your ancestors can be encoded in your DNA, and thus your health and your behaviors? Well, this is also a wound that needs to be healed, and the way to heal it is to truly dive into the pain and trauma that your ancestors experienced. You have to feel and express their pain. The late spiritual teacher Stephen Levine called this "The pain that ends the pain."

Start by creating a genogram. You do this by making a diagram of your family. Put in your parents, your siblings, your grandparents, your aunts and uncles, your cousins, and your great-grandparents. Find out as much as you can about each one. Was anyone mentally ill or institutionalized? What are the family secrets? Did anyone suffer a stillbirth? Was anyone a convicted felon? An alcoholic? An addict? Were there any out-of-wedlock children who were raised as siblings of their mothers? (This was common practice in the past—to protect a woman from the shame of an unwed pregnancy.) Did anyone die in childbirth? Have a severe accident? Die in the Holocaust? You get the picture. Remember that family traumas are carried in our DNA and passed down to us. We empaths are particularly sensitive to the unhealed wounds of our family tree. And rather than passing them on blindly, it's very helpful to address them directly.

One of my patients, whom I'll call Samantha, did this exercise to see where all the sexual abuse came from in her family. Her father had been a pedophile. And she had been warned by her mother never to play with certain friends who were "his type." Obviously her mother was protecting this man throughout Samantha's childhood—making it Samantha's "job" to curate her playmates. Eventually Samantha's father was jailed for his predatory sexual behavior. He was found guilty of abusing a neighborhood girl. But he also abused Samantha's sister. Sadly, Samantha's mother bailed him out and kept protecting him.

While Samantha recognized that sexual predators were a problem in her family—actually on both sides of her family—she thought she could protect any children of her own by marrying a prominent doctor. They went on to have two daughters, and even with all the paranoia about evading predators, one of her husband's astute colleagues ended up sexually abusing one of them. And the other was raped at knifepoint when she was 16.

Samantha was not conscious of the power of inherited trauma until she came to see me for the first time following a slight heart attack at the age of 52. When she learned, she became determined to heal not only her body, but her life. She felt compelled to create a genogram to further explore her family history. Seeing all of it laid out in front of her helped enormously to illuminate the legacy. And it also brought her a great deal of peace and closure as she realized that the only thing she could do with all of this was feel it—expressing her righteous anger and deep sadness, her despair and horror, and her pain and compassion. She had to feel it, forgive it, and release it. Samantha happens to have a deep Christian faith and a very strong relationship with Mother Mary, and this has helped her a great deal in this process. Believe it or not, she is a very happy and fulfilled woman at this point. And her daughters have benefited greatly from her clarity and peace in their own lives. Forgiving herself for not protecting her sister or her daughters was the biggest healer. As she worked through the pain, she realized that as a young mother she didn't have the resources, the support from her family, or the knowledge to prevent the abuse. Though this is a very dramatic example of sexual trauma and predatory behavior passed down in families, it sure gets to the point.

The bottom line is this: When we can name something, we can often change it. On an energetic and global level, the work Samantha did to heal this helped stop the pattern. Neither of her daughters went on to have children. And so, in this case, that legacy will no longer be passed on to anyone. A pretty stark way to end a pattern—and not one that any of us would care to repeat.

Luckily, there's a much easier way: Acknowledge your lineage. The good, the bad, the ugly. I remember when I found out that there were alcoholics on both sides of my family—and most likely narcissism as well. I realized that I shared many of the characteristics of adult grandchildren of alcoholics such as perfectionism, tendency to be a people pleaser, walking on eggshells around the unacknowledged emotions of others—characteristics that mirror those of an empath. I have done a great deal of recovery work on this. I've also concentrated on healing my own patterns of overcompensation and agreeableness, which were so evident in my father. He was a master at smoothing things over, taking the high road, and being optimistic and fun—almost always. Through my work of clearly seeing these patterns in myself, I have eliminated the ones that are too costly in terms of my time and my health. I say no far more often. And I take time for myself. This conscious change has also helped with other family members. I have been able to assist not only my siblings, but also nieces and nephews to exit dark patterns handed down in the family lineage.

To heal our past, we must first become aware of how Darkness works. Shining a light on it is the first step. And then forgiving ourselves and being unconditionally loving—and also changing our behavior, if necessary—is the next step to clean up the legacy for good.

Being acutely aware of your legacy, resolve to not mindlessly repeat it—what Carl Jung refers to as the unacknowledged unconscious patterns coming to us as fate. I have done everything in my power to change these things not only for my own health, but also so that this pattern doesn't get handed down to my own daughters and grandchildren.

TRANSFORMING EMPATHY INTO A SUPERPOWER

Once we learn that there's nothing inherently wrong with us, and know how to simply be with our pain, care for the wounded little kid inside, and what to do to heal— then we stop looking to others for validation. We stop trying to please others as a way to feel safe and connected. Instead we become unstoppable. Not because we are no longer sensitive—that never goes away—but because we finally "get" how energy works. We remember who we really are—the lighthouses of heaven on earth. But we can't be effective as light carriers if we are always allowing other people to bring us down. That's one part of it. But there's another.

The light we carry quite literally causes Darkness to recede. But before receding, it often tries to bring us down. Or cause us to doubt ourselves and stay small and safe. Let's go back to the TSA agent at LaGuardia. That woman and her colleague were very far from feeling light, compassion, and love. And as an empath, I felt that lack of light. Physically. Acutely. The energy differential between us was enormous. I noted it. And then turned my attention to more uplifting things. Knowing all the while that my very presence was healing to the energy there.

Here's the deal. When another individual is completely disconnected from their well-being and their joy, this has absolutely nothing to do with you on any level. You didn't attract this. You are not responsible for it. The only thing you are responsible for is your own energy field. And when you learn how to pay attention to that—and only that—you're free. Simple. Not easy.

Chapter 9

THE CAUSES OF HEALTH

We've covered a great deal of information about healing the emotional body, so now let's move on to the physical body. Whether or not you are currently living with a vampire, you need to know that there's a lot you can do physically to create better health and make yourself more "vampire-proof," though eventually you'll want to stop any and all life energy leakage from your body to theirs.

Before we jump into specific practices, which we'll do in the next chapter, I want to remind you that flourishing in a physical body is about far more than having a perfect diet and exercise routine. I've treated many people over the years who have followed almost perfect diets—all whole organic foods—who still got sick. And those for whom exercise is religion are not immune either. Plus, conversely, we all know people in their 90s who are in excellent health who still smoke and drink alcohol regularly. And never worry about their diet or exercise routines. Never did. So what is the common thread that ties this all together? How one uses their life energy. And how well they practice what Dr. Mario Martinez calls "the causes of health":

1. **Elevated cognition:** Thinking positive and uplifting thoughts and seeking out good news.

2. **Exalted emotions:** Feeling ecstatic emotions regularly; engaging in things that bring you joy, inspiration, delight, awe, love, devotion, and pleasure.

3. **Righteous anger:** Expressing and acting on the justifiable anger that comes from pain caused without regard for your own or another's innocence and humanity.

And I would add a fourth cause to this list:

4. **Expressed emotions:** Not suppressing emotions—good or bad—to the point where they manifest as illness in the body. While this is similar to the righteous anger point above, I believe that it applies to all emotions.

ELEVATED COGNITION

The idea of thinking positive thoughts is pretty straightforward. You've probably heard the phrase "Choose the thought that feels better." Seems simple enough, right? And it is simple, but it's not always easy. Here's how it works. Let's say you have applied for a job that you really want, and you find yourself worrying that you won't get it. Your mind swirls around with thoughts like *There are so many people who are more qualified than I am.* Or *I wasn't at*

my best when I wrote that cover letter. There's just no chance.
To choose the thought that feels better—and this is where
it gets tough—you must catch yourself diving into negativity and stop yourself. Once you recognize the negativity, you can consciously replace that negative thought
with one of higher vibration. An example would be *Well,
someone has to get that job. Why not me?* Or *If I don't get this
job, it means that there is something better for me.* You get the
idea. And yes—this takes practice because, as I've already
mentioned, 90 percent of our thoughts stem from our subconscious mind and childhood or past-life programming.
And the vast majority of those thoughts are negative.

Here's a technique that might help you as you start
to shift your thought patterns. Right now, sit down and
think about something you really want and write down
all the reasons you think you can't have it. If you want
a relationship, you might find yourself thinking, *I'm too
ugly.* Or *I'm too crazy.* Or *I can't imagine anyone falling for me.*
Get familiar with the patterns of thought that come up
for you. That's all you have to do right now. Start listening
to your inner dialogue. Note it. Understand it. The more
conscious attention you pay to it, the more likely you are
to notice it in the moment. And that's when you have the
power to stop it in its tracks. Even if you don't necessarily
believe the opposite of it, you can argue with it. You can
do a reality check on it. Are you really too ugly to have a
relationship? No. You're not. Look around you.

You can also do an instant turnaround on these negative thoughts by congratulating yourself and finding yourself right for having them. I learned this from spiritual
teacher Matt Kahn. It's similar to what we did in Chapter 6
when guilt arose—and just like that, it works like a charm.
So let's say you've caught yourself thinking that you're too

ugly or too old to have a relationship. Instead of arguing with yourself or doing a reality check, you just say, "Wow! Congratulations! No one has ever thought like this before! You're doing great!" You don't beat yourself up; you just choose an instant elevated cognition.

I've taught this on my Hay House radio show regularly when people share their fears about their health, their life, their relationships, their children, etc. And it instantly turns negativity into elevated cognition and the exalted emotion of humor. Catch yourself in the middle of a negative thought. And then celebrate how well you're doing it. Works like a charm.

The important thing with these techniques is that you can't judge yourself for having these thoughts. You need to notice and accept them, because if you simply ignore them, you are in essence resisting them—acting like they don't exist. And what we resist persists. Every thought we have is there for a reason. Negative thoughts arise from our shadow self, the disowned parts of ourselves that we have too often been judged harshly for and now feel we have to hide. Which is why so many of those thoughts aren't even fully conscious. The more you beat yourself up for having negative thoughts, the more they persist.

Every thought you think also has an accompanying vibration. Thoughts and words that are imbued with beauty, compassion, humor, and inspiration have a far more positive effect on the body than worst-case-scenario thoughts such as *Everyone in my family gets cancer. It's just a matter of time before it happens to me.* Or *All the good men are taken. I'll be single for the rest of my life.*

So that's the first part of elevated cognition, but elevated cognition also means that you seek out good news. To do this, you carefully curate the kinds of literature, movies, and media that you watch, listen to, and read. Just like our thoughts, every sound we hear and every image we see has a vibration.

The physical effects of words and images have even been proved experimentally. An article published in the journal *Psychology & Health* in 1988 recounted a study on this topic done by David C. McClelland of Harvard University and Carol Kirshnit of Loyola University of Chicago. In it, medical students were shown two different movies and the levels of an antibody known as IgA were measured in their saliva samples. Levels of IgA in the body correspond with the strength of our immune system: High levels are associated with a strong immune system and low levels are a sign of weakened immunity. In the experiment, McClelland wanted to see if simply watching and hearing certain subject matter could affect immunity. One movie was about war and the other featured Mother Teresa doing her work in Calcutta.

After watching the destruction of war, the students' immune system levels plummeted. And after watching Mother Teresa, their antibody levels rose—including those of students who didn't hold any particular spiritual beliefs. The physical body responds to that which is life-affirming and associated with healthy affiliation with others—those things that make life worth living.

Practice elevated cognition by choosing uplifting or funny movies or television shows. Choose books with uplifting, inspiring, fascinating, or funny messages. Become media savvy and follow the money behind the mainstream news. Remember that Darkness feeds on your fear and anger, so stop feeding it. That doesn't mean you bury your head in the sand. It just means that you use your own power to curate the things that you allow to enter your mind, spirit, and body. You become a force for good—not another pawn in a machine that runs on greed, fear, and powerlessness.

EXALTED EMOTIONS

In his book *The Big Leap*, psychologist Dr. Gay Hendricks points out that we all learn an "upper limit" to how much joy, pleasure, and happiness—and other exalted emotions—we're supposed to feel. Our families and cultures teach us that there is a limit to how much joy we are allowed to experience. No doubt you've heard someone say, "You're having way too much fun over there"—if you are laughing and enjoying yourself. Or "Don't break your arm patting yourself on the back." Or "Don't toot your own horn." All of these phrases speak to the fact that many of us—especially highly sensitive individuals—learn early on to put a ceiling on our joy so that others will feel more comfortable around us. After all, if someone is angry or sad, we instinctively know that our own joy and pleasure will irritate them and make them feel uncomfortable. Over time, we internalize the idea that there really is such a thing as "having too much fun." And then, unfortunately, the only way we can loosen up and uncouple those "buzzkill" frontal lobe inhibitory circuits in our brains is through culturally approved drugs or alcohol.

The truth is that we are born with an enormous capacity for joy and pleasure. Watch any two-year-old if you doubt this. I took a walk with my then 20-month-old granddaughter a while back. We came to a little wooden bridge on the trail, with a slight elevation above the rest of the trail. She delighted in jumping off this little bridge back onto the trail. Over and over again. Each time exclaiming "Ready, set . . ." and then jumping. Just watching her delight was uplifting and joyous. I remembered that long ago I used to enjoy turning somersaults underwater in the farm pond on the property where I grew up. I'd spend what I referred to as timeless time just being in the water and enjoying the sun, the water, and my ability to move. As the years passed, however, I lost that capacity to lose myself in timeless time and live in the moment. Fortunately I've learned how to go back there. And so can you. It is our native land, after all.

We all have the capacity to feel more joy and pleasure. But you first have to notice when you are, in fact, feeling joy. So begin to pay attention to when you feel happy or joyous. Or when you experience something exalted. Purposely start looking for what brings you joy. Pay attention to the beauty of flowers. How does a gorgeous window box make you feel? And what about music? For me, there is no quicker way to reach the heart than listening to—or playing—a beautiful piece of music. So often we find ourselves putting off feeling joy and pleasure until "later." When we have time. The thing is, you must make time. Because feeling exalted emotions takes no time at all. You simply have to be present with the joy and beauty that are all around.

I recommend making exalted emotions a regular part of your day. Create Spotify playlists of soaring music that touches your soul and then listen to a few songs before you go to bed at night. I love listening to Lee Carroll's channel Kryon on YouTube. I also listen to Matt Kahn's YouTube lectures. In addition, I'm a big fan of TED Talks. They are always inspiring and uplifting.

Another very practical way to practice exalted emotions is to create a list of affirmations and say them out loud when you get up in the morning or when you go to bed. Don't just mouth the words. Embody the affirmation as you say it. Feel it. Become an Academy Award–winning actor in your own life. Speak the words as though they are true right now. That alone will draw a higher vibration to you. As Michael Beckwith of the Agape International Spiritual Center in Culver City, California, says, "Affirmations don't make something happen. They make something welcome." Here's an example: "I am a radiant, powerful human being who lives life with joy and pleasure. I am a magnet for good." When you say this and then something really good happens to you, you will notice it. I suggest you even write it down and have the courage to share your good fortune or your good feeling with someone else who celebrates you. Remember, part of building self-esteem is feeling worthy of having the good things in your life celebrated.

Over time, practicing exalted emotions and elevated cognition will draw to you an entirely new tribe of people with whom you can freely share your good and be celebrated and uplifted—not put down. As a result, your entire life will become transformed and you won't have to dim your light anymore in order to make others feel more comfortable. Remember the phrase, "When we dim our light to make others feel more comfortable, the whole world gets darker." Do the opposite. Shine ever brighter!!

One more tip. Gay Hendricks came up with what he calls the "Ultimate Success Mantra" as a good place to start. Every morning before you get out of bed, say the following: "I expand in abundance, success, and love every day as I inspire those around me to do the same." This mantra works on the subconscious mind, which doesn't have a way to push up against the word *expand*. So it just follows the instructions. Change it however you wish—putting in anything you'd like to expand—maybe physical health, strength, or beauty, you name it. Eventually that ceiling on your exalted emotions will lift and you'll be able to feel even more. But just a word of caution: Our ability to feel maximum amounts of joy is related to our willingness to feel and move through our emotional pain. You can't have one without the other. I'll get to that more below.

RIGHTEOUS ANGER

Remember the monks we talked about in Chapter 4? They turned to compassion instead of expressing anger, and they got diabetes in the process. This is similar to what an empath does. Instead of leaving or fighting, the empath tries to live according to spiritual practices such as loving-kindness, empathic joy (celebrating the success of others), compassion (wanting to end the suffering of all beings), and equanimity (living in harmony and peace of mind). This certainly seems not only reasonable, but also laudable. But there's that big problem of our immune systems having morals. They won't allow us to bypass righteous anger when our innocence or that of a loved one is threatened. The proper response in these situations is anger—and action. And if you don't act on this anger, you become drained, tired, and stressed, with all the corresponding rises in stress hormones.

Let's look at an example. You see that your child is about to be harmed by an adult. Your response is to get angry with the abuser and get your child out of harm's way. You don't say, "We are all one." Or "May all beings be free of suffering." Or make excuses for the abuser, "He had a difficult childhood so I understand why he's taking it out on my child." No. Doing any of these things would be a crime. Instead you do what needs to be done to protect your child. And your body acts accordingly: pumping you full of the necessary energizing stress hormones to handle the situation. Once the situation has been handled, those hormone levels return to homeostasis.

To maintain your health and peace of mind, you must tap into your righteous anger at allowing yourself to be used and abused. In the instance of vampire relationships, this means that you must either get out of or minimize time spent with the other person. And you must realize that being spiritual and unconditionally loving does not mean putting up with abuse of any kind. This is how marriage and relationship therapist Dr. Pat Allen puts it in her book *It's a Man's World and a Woman's Universe*: "If your mate is not overall 51 percent valuable, you cannot stay with them and remain healthy. Being in a toxic relationship may be a sign of unconditional love, but it's also a sign that you love them more than yourself. That is a sign of mental illness."

Of course if you happen to be born into a family or culture where self-sacrifice and over-giving are rewarded and it is the only way you've ever been noticed or received attention, it's not really mental illness. It's an adaptive strategy to a pathological situation. Happily, once you notice this in yourself, you can tap into your inner power to change the situation.

As an empath and a healer, it's often hard to believe that any anger is justified. But you need to know that it's not only justified, it's absolutely essential for your long-term health and well-being. Let me give you an example from my own life.

This past summer I had the pleasure of going back to my childhood home for a visit. And as you well know, nothing pushes your buttons like your immediate family. Each time I go home, I learn a lot about myself, and heal another layer. I have done a lot of work bringing to consciousness the lessons I came to learn in the particular family I chose. And I'm fortunate enough to have a good relationship with all of my family members. My biggest challenge has been the fact that, as the black sheep of the family, I just don't fit into the activities and interests they share. Because they are wonderful people who I truly love and enjoy, I've felt flawed in some way—as in *What is wrong with me that I just can't seem to enjoy participating in four sports a day?* I have neither the body nor the spirit of a competitive athlete. But this is what my family most honors and celebrates—particularly my mother, who is still thriving. I knew that this trip could be a wonderful opportunity for clarity and further healing. After all, at this point, I have pretty much proven my worth—and no one is judging me except me!

This summer I took my good friend Hope Matthews, who has been my Pilates teacher and intuitive movement healer for 15 years, to keep me company. Hope is very familiar with the emotional patterns that have affected my physical body, many of which I have changed for the better over the years, so much so that my body works better now than it did 20 years ago. Because of this and because she is another old-soul empath, Hope was the perfect person to bear witness to my interactions with my family and to validate my emotional reactions—especially any negative ones.

Sure enough, an opportunity to express true righteous anger arose. My brothers, their wives, my niece and her husband, and my mother had all planned to have dinner together on a Saturday night and then watch the movie *A Dog's Purpose*. They all have dogs and the movie is precious. On Friday night—while enjoying a hilarious get-together at a local restaurant—we set up the next evening. My mother would prepare a chicken dish, my sister-in-law would make popcorn, I'd make salad. We'd eat around six. Then watch the movie. It was going to be wonderful.

The next evening, at just before six, my brother mentioned that there was a singer who was performing down at a local bar. He said he might go. Then he helped me wash the salad. Six o'clock came. Dinner was ready—and my brother and his wife (the one who said she'd make popcorn) were nowhere to be found. They had just vanished. Without saying a word.

My sister-in-law sent me a brief video of the singer. I responded, "Lovely. But didn't we have a plan to eat dinner and then watch the movie?" I then texted my brother. "Are you coming home?" He texted back, "I had a choice between two things I wanted to do. And I chose to stay here and watch the singer." I was furious. Now here's the important part. I *knew* that I was furious. And I knew that my anger was totally justified. I had a witness who had been there when we had made plans the night before. I didn't feel crazy. I was clear as a bell. And really angry. I allowed myself to feel my anger in every cell of my body. I knew that this was an important part of maintaining my health. That this was white-hot righteous anger.

I texted my missing brother back and said, "You get to do whatever you want. But I am angry that you didn't tell me . . . or anyone else."

We all sat down and had our dinner without my missing brother and his wife. And I sat there knowing full well that I was not going to just smooth this over. After dinner, my brother texted me back: "You're right. I should have told you."

And with that, my anger melted like fog in the mist. He apologized. I felt complete. I knew that his wife had decided to go hear the singer and forgo the dinner. And he was feeling caught between her desires and the rest of us. Normal stuff. Happens every day. No problem. All he had to do was just let me know. The next day he gave me a hug and said, "Thank you for understanding." In the past, I would have gone right to understanding, deep-sixing my righteous anger and messing up my hormones in the process. This time I knew better.

EXPRESSED EMOTIONS

As you can probably tell, emotions—such as righteous anger—are not just pesky problems to overcome; they are signals from your body regarding your needs. If these emotions are not heeded—both in their expression and in action taken because of them—then they will change the course of your life.

Expressing and acting on positive emotions will steer you in the direction you want to go. They will bring beauty and support into your life. Think about it. If you feel overwhelmed with gratitude and you pay attention to this, you know that you are doing something or interacting with someone who brings joy into your life, so you will look for more of that. If you express that gratitude—especially if it is to someone else—you will call forth more of the situations that inspired that gratitude in the first place.

Most empaths don't have a problem noticing and expressing the positive emotions; however, they do have problems with negative emotions. But to live a healthy life, this needs to stop. Emotions that are left unexpressed and unacted upon often manifest as illness in the body.

I can remember coming downstairs when I was a young teen and if I wasn't the picture of cheerful happiness, my father would make me go back upstairs and come down again when I had a smile on my face and a spring in my step. While there is nothing inherently wrong with teaching a child how to modulate emotions in a more positive direction, the problem that existed here is that I was not allowed to express negative emotions at all. And so I believed that there was something wrong with any emotion that wasn't happiness and cheeriness. As a result, I buried my true emotions and the needs they were designed to help me fulfill. Instead, I decided that my anger, sadness, and grief were signs that I was a flawed human being and that these emotions had to be suppressed at all costs. So of course they went into my body. I developed migraines, plantar fasciitis, and astigmatism.

It wasn't until years later that I discovered that every emotion signifies a genuine need that isn't being met (at least for an empath—not necessarily a vampire). I didn't understand that my emotions were my God-given guidance system designed to help me identify and then get my needs met.

When you're feeling negative emotions, you need to make sure that you don't suppress them. When you've lost a child, been through a devastating divorce, or the death of a beloved friend or spouse, you simply must surrender to the healing balm of movement, sound, and tears—the body's innate way to heal deep pain. There is no other way to heal pain and move into joy than to feel it and move through it. Eventually you have to wail and moan—shed tears—and then surrender to a Higher Power. Otherwise, all this energy will get stuck in your body and result in all kinds of health problems.

And this isn't just true with present-day emotions. You have to deal with the events and situations that hurt you in the past. Trust me, these areas of pain will not get better through mere positive thinking, affirmations, and vision boards. Think of your health like you would a wall covered in old wallpaper that you're going to redo. You won't get a good result by just slapping up the new stuff over the old. You first have to strip the old paper off and repair the surface of the wall. Only then will you have the proper surface for the brand-new paper. It's the same thing with the grief, pain, and loss that we have from childhood and past lives.

Unresolved pain and trauma from childhood or from your family genetic line will continue to operate below the surface—creating the opposite of a healthy, joyful life. And any attempt to think positively or change your beliefs without actually identifying the source of the pain and allowing that pain to be felt and released simply won't work. But neither is it healthy to create a shrine to your grief and expect everyone to worship it. For example, you can't create a shrine from your child's bedroom after they pass away. Doing this will also enshrine your pain and cause you to become a vampire yourself.

So, expressing emotion—sounds easy enough, doesn't it?

Well, it is and it isn't. It is because it's a natural part of who we are, but it isn't because most of us have programmed into ourselves the need to suppress our emotions. With this topic, again, it's a matter of recognizing when they occur and encouraging them.

I'll never forget being in an Anne Wilson Schaef "Living in Process" workshop back in the early '90s. The format was that we simply sat "with ourselves," and when someone had something to say, they said it. Very often, the things that were shared triggered other people in the group. When they got triggered or felt something emotional come up, they would lie down on one of the mattresses that were strewn about the room and allow themselves to simply feel. They would go all the way into the feeling—making the sounds they needed to make and the movements that felt healing. Meanwhile, someone would go and sit with them. That person would *not* touch them; they would merely hand them tissues as needed.

At the time, this felt a whole lot like the labor and delivery area of the hospital in which I worked. It felt like we were all midwives for those who were birthing more conscious parts of themselves and leaving the pain behind. And then it was my turn. I had been observing people wailing on the mattresses for about seven days feeling like I had it all together and they didn't. Poor things. At the time, my colleagues and I had gone to this workshop to deal with what we thought was our "codependency"—a vague term that I no longer use to describe myself. But at the time, it was all we had, and we knew that Anne was skilled in this area. We mostly came to have help with a formal intervention, which I was eager to get on with.

The time for our intervention came, and Anne sat the four of us down in an inner circle surrounded by all the other 50 participants. The first part of an intervention is that you tell the person how much you love and care about them. I started by telling my colleague how much it meant to me that she showed up at the hospital when I was in labor with my second child and parked my car so that my husband and I could go into the hospital together. And I burst into tears. Having a female colleague do something like this for me was so rare I could barely take it in.

And the memory of it moved me to tears. Anne said, "Do you want to lie down and see what comes up?" I quickly regained my composure and choked back my tears. After all, we were doing an intervention. Who was I to interrupt the purpose of the meeting with my own emotions? Nope. I pushed those feelings right back down—something I had mastered very well in childhood and later in medical school and residency. And then Anne said, "You're so tired." And with that, the dam burst. And I laid on that mattress and wailed for at least an hour.

I had ancient sounds coming out of me that were like the women at the Wailing Wall in Jerusalem. My witness self—the part of all of us that simply watches us outside of time and space—was intrigued. Who knew I could make those sounds? And during the process, I found myself weeping for all the times that I never got to rest. And then I went backward in time. And wept for my own mother. And then her mother—my grandmother Ruth—who was orphaned at the age of three when her own mother died. And then a trap door opened someplace in my consciousness and I went down into it—deeper and deeper into a place called "the pain of all women." And I wailed for all the women who ever lost a baby in childbirth, or lost their own mother, or who never got to rest. And that place was just endless. As was my wailing. Soon the entire room—men and women—were all down on mattresses wailing. When it was finally done, I realized that I had been born to transform this pain—the pain of women—into joy. I knew it in my cells. And I knew that I had to start with me.

Since that time, there have been many other occasions when I have felt deep emotions arise. And have then gone into my bedroom, shut the door, lay down, and just let the feelings come. Sometimes it's rage. Sometimes grief.

Sometimes deep sadness. But here's the thing: When you allow yourself to go all the way in and all the way out—with movement, sound, and tears—your body will clear the trauma from your DNA. Nothing else is required. We are born equipped to do this. All babies do this naturally. Sometimes you just need to cry it out.

The very first time you allow yourself to do this, you may feel as though if you allow yourself to truly go all the way down into the abyss of pain, you will never ever get out. Trust me—you'll get out. But that's why it's often helpful to have a trusted friend just sit with you as a witness. A word of caution: Your witness is *not* allowed to hug you or try to "talk you through it." That will stop your process. The reason we often feel so compelled to hug another who is in pain is that their pain triggers our own. So we hug them to stop *ourselves* from feeling fully. Don't do this.

Many times, a deep emotion will arise when it is not convenient to let yourself go all the way into it. In that case, you just say to yourself, "Don't worry. I'll get back to you." And then make a point to attend to that deep emotion as soon as you can. It will still be there.

When we allow ourselves to feel our deepest pain, we also have access to our most ebullient joy. Very often, you will find yourself laughing hysterically after a deep emotional release. Your cork just naturally rises to the top.

Also after allowing yourself to feel and release old stuck emotions, you will lose weight and look much younger. This work literally turns back the clock. Because you are no longer hauling burdens around from the past.

As Woody Allen put it in his movie *Manhattan*, "I can't express anger. That's one of the problems I have. I grow a tumor instead." It is my hope, in writing this book, that you won't have to grow a tumor in order to finally feel your rage, grief, and anger.

THE RIGHT HEALTH CARE FOR YOU

Before we move on to particular healing practices, there are a few things I want you to know about your health care. First and foremost, chances are really good that you are highly sensitive to standard medications—maybe even aspirin. The usual dose will be too high and if you follow the recommendations on the jar, you'll likely have adverse effects. One of my colleagues who works as a professional intuitive recently was prescribed 10 milligrams of prednisone for a pinched nerve problem. Generally, people are given much higher doses of prednisone—up to 60 milligrams or more—at the onset of a severe problem in order to stop the pain and inflammation quickly. Then they taper down gradually over the next several days or weeks. But my friend said she felt anxious and psychotic for two days following that one low dose. The pain medication she was prescribed also affected her adversely. So she stopped taking it. I hear this sort of thing repeatedly.

Generally speaking, highly sensitive people do far better with healing approaches based on quantum energy, not chemical and surgical intervention. Homeopathy, flower essences, acupuncture, massage, herbs, prayer, yoga, Pilates, chiropractic, medical intuition, and Divine Love healings—I consider all of these to be actual health care because all of these things interact with the energy field of the body first.

Problems in the energy body can be addressed long before they manifest in the physical body, and this is how you maintain and regain health. Years ago, I had my first reading with the renowned medical intuitive Caroline Myss. During the reading, she said, "Your heart rate has changed over the past five years. You are a rescue addict; do you hear me? You have to get this under control."

Given that heart disease "runs in my family," I took this information very seriously indeed and began to look at the patterns in my life that were causing me to feel such a need to rescue everyone in my medical practice and personal life. Was there anything wrong with my heart that conventional medicine could detect? No. My EKG, resting pulse rate, blood pressure, and cholesterol were absolutely fine. They still are. What wasn't fine was my life energy. I was leaking it all over the place without replenishing it regularly for myself. Years later, my heart is better than ever. But only because I worked on the pattern of life energy leakage.

Conventional medicine is excellent for accidents, trauma, joint replacements, and life-threatening emergencies. But it falls far short when it comes to maintaining health or treating chronic conditions. Modern medicine is based on a war-like belief system that is obsolete and badly in need of upgrading. Doctors now often believe that there's a "pill for every ill." When it comes to cancer or infectious disease the approach is radiate, cut out, or poison the tumor. They aim to eradicate every germ with antibiotics. But the approach of medicine today has failed miserably when it comes to the most common chronic diseases like diabetes, arthritis, and cancer. It is well documented that medical errors are the third leading cause of death in the United States. So I recommend that you establish relationships with real healers in your community. And schedule regular sessions to stay healthy.

Chapter 10

PHYSICAL HEALING POST-VAMPIRE

Now that you know what it takes—from the big-picture perspective—to get and stay healthy, let's look at some practices that are designed to heal exactly what your vampire relationship has taken away from you.

HEALING WITH DIVINE LOVE

The first technique I want to tell you about isn't vampire-specific healing. It's a one-size-fits-all approach to health and healing that I believe everyone—especially highly sensitive individuals—should know about. And that is Divine Love healing. If you've read my last couple of books, you'll probably recognize this, but I need to include it again here because it's such a powerful healing technique. So bear with me if you've already heard this.

I first learned about Divine Love several years ago from Bob Fritchie, a retired aerospace engineer. This process invokes the power of the Creator and Divine Love in order to effect changes in matter and circumstance. I know this may be hard to believe, but set your ego aside for a moment. While modern science and medicine may not be able to explain the effects of this practice right now, just remember that a lobotomy used to be a cure for depression. And heroin used to be administered as a cough suppressant. Science and medicine may one day catch up to the healing power of Divine Love.

Before we begin, let me say that Divine Love is *not* the same as personal love. Personal love is the kind that can be so deadly to us empaths. We have the capacity to love others at the expense of ourselves. But Divine Love doesn't reside in one person—and it doesn't stop with one person. It is available for free to anyone who can answer "yes" to the following two questions: 1. Do you believe in God or a Higher Power? and 2. Do you really want to get well?

Okay—so how do you use Divine Love?

You simply ask—in the form of a petition—for Divine Love to work through you. It's like plugging yourself into a higher vibration that is always available to you.

Here's the process:

1. Sit with your arms and legs uncrossed. The body is a battery—and crossing arms or legs will short it out.

2. Remove all jewelry.

3. Put your feet flat on the floor.

4. Say the following all-purpose petition I learned from Bob. "With my Spirit and the help of the Loving Angels of the Light, I focus Divine Love throughout my system. I ask my Spirit to identify every cause and

every situation that separates me from the Creator. And now ask that all of these be removed with Divine Love according to the Creator's Will."

5. Now draw in your breath through your nose. (This draws in your intent.) Hold for a count of four. Then pulse out through your nostrils, like you are clearing your nose. This sends the intent out into the universe.

6. Now simply sit and focus your attention gently on your thymus gland, which is located deep to your breast bone. This is the place in the body where Divine Love enters and is then distributed throughout the body.

I like to set a timer for two minutes when I do a Divine Love meditation. I say the petition, pulse my breath, then set the timer on my phone. I pay attention to images, thoughts, feelings, and also songs that occur to me during that time frame. I'm amazed by the information that comes in, often in vivid pictures with a soundtrack. This approach gives me a great deal of intuitive information that I use in daily life. And when I do petitions with my colleague Diane Grover, with whom I've worked for decades, she often gets information for me that I can't get for myself. And vice versa. For example, one time when we were doing Divine Love meditations for each other, she "saw" a man I'd been working with right in the middle of her meditation—and he looked and acted just like Gollum ("my precious!") from *Lord of the Rings*. I later had a couple of dreams about him that confirmed what she saw, and that was the information I needed to stop working with him. Later, I found out that he is (surprise!) a first-class vampire.

When doing the petitions, you can simply say the generic ones above or you can say a specific petition for a specific problem. For example, "With my Spirit, I focus Divine Love throughout my system, I acknowledge my headache, and I ask that this be healed, with Divine Love, according to the Creator's Will." Just use one symptom at a time.

Very often I gather family members or friends together to send Divine Love healing to someone in need, like a family member or friend. We use a free conference call number; everyone calls in, and then I say the petition and set the timer. Afterward, everyone weighs in on what they experienced. And very often the person who is receiving the healing energy feels it profoundly. For example, a couple of years ago, my mother began to have difficulty exercising. She'd feel weak and short of breath, which was very unusual since she has been a hiker for decades and is very fit. Her cardiac workup was normal—with a normal EKG. One day she called me and said her heart rate was only about 40. We couldn't figure out what was going on. She flew out to the Mayo Clinic in Scottsdale, Arizona, where my sister was living at the time. It turns out that Mom needed a pacemaker. But since her problem was intermittent, no one had diagnosed it. Her cardiologist was a fantastic woman who had all the residents come and listen to my mother's heart, telling them, "Pay attention—this is what a strong, healthy, unmedicated heart sounds like." In any case, her pacemaker insertion was scheduled for the following Monday, and she had to be in the hospital all weekend. With a dangerously low heart rate. I gathered everyone together on the phone for a Divine Love healing. It was profoundly healing for all of us. I "saw" my father (who died long ago), dancing on Mom's bed and cheering her on. I also heard the song "Swing Low, Sweet Chariot." Other family members, moved to tears, told my mother a lot of celebratory things they felt and saw. My mother was overcome with profound peace. No one knew what was going to happen. My mother had signed a "do not resuscitate" order. That Monday, she got her pacemaker and is now back to her usual hiking and other activities. The ability to gather a group together to send and receive Divine Love is a profoundly practical and moving practice that I highly recommend.

Divine Love is being used with specific protocols by Bob Fritchie via his organization, the World Service Institute, a registered 501(c)(3) nonprofit organization. Currently he is working with helping drug addicts, and so far he has a 60 percent success rate with those who can answer "yes" to the two questions I mentioned above. He has also documented how Divine Love has healed various conditions including cancer.

Interestingly, we've also realized that you can preemptively heal yourself from the effects of low-quality food and water using Divine Love. You can in essence "treat" the food and water with Divine Love. Before eating or drinking, just say, "I infuse this food with Divine Love so that it contributes to my well-being." Now draw in your breath and pulse it. Done. This will help counteract any negative aspects of the food or water. Will it make it clean and organic? No. But it will infuse it with the love of the Creator, which will make it more healthful.

As you start your day and go out into the world, send Divine Love out in front of you—and behind you as well. It's the very best kind of protection. Here's all you have to do. You get out of bed—or remain in bed—and say out loud or in your head, "I now send Divine Love out into the world in front of me, all around me, and behind me. I am Divinely protected as I go out into the world today." Draw your breath in. Hold it. And pulse it out. Repeat as desired.

HEALTH MAINTENANCE

Healing and maintaining your health after a vampire relationship is all about bringing down stress and reducing the inflammation that leads to the health issues we talked about in Chapter 4. While these practices are good for everyone, they are essential for people recovering from vampire abuse.

One thing to note: Do not expect too much of yourself until you're able to set good boundaries with your vampire. Implementing these practices may keep you healthier in a bad relationship, but they can't compete with the overwhelming amount of stress hormones that you experience in a vampire relationship.

I've tried to make a list of simple practices that you can implement in your life without too much stress—because again, this is about combating stress and its associated inflammation. I'd recommend that you read through this list and pick a couple of things you can do easily. Choose the ones that work for you now. And remember, success breeds more success. And baby steps work far better than doing some kind of crash course in healthy living.

Start and End Your Day Consciously

Having an intention for your day can change the way you interact with the world, which is great for reducing stress. One great way to do this is by combining the power of meditation and imagination.

Meditation has been the focus of a great deal of research lately, and it has been shown to help everything from depression to anxiety to weight gain to PTSD. The source of all this healing is you. When you focus your mind and allow your thoughts to become still, you naturally tap into your true essence—which is Divine, powerful, and made of love.

Meditation doesn't have to be hard. Simply start with 10 minutes per day. When you wake up is best because it sets the tone for the day. Here's a quick meditation that I like to do.

Set a timer for 10 minutes. Sit with your back straight. (You don't need to be in any unusual position.) Close your eyes. Now imagine a cord running from your belly button into the center of the earth. Imagine earth's energy coming back up to your belly button. Now imagine a cord going from your belly button up into the sky—bringing heaven down into your body. You are now fully connected. Now for the next 10 minutes, focus on your belly button. Notice what images, feelings, and colors come to mind. When the timer is done, write down what you saw or felt. That's it.

After I do this, I imagine how I want my day to go. I spend a couple of minutes imagining everything that can go right, and then in the evening before I go to bed, I ask myself, "What can I learn from today?" And I write the answers down.

I learned this A.M. and P.M. technique from Joseph Clough, a master hypnotist who teaches people how to send messages to their unconscious minds to reach their full potential. The imagination part at the beginning of the day works because your mind can't tell the difference between what is real and what is not, so experiencing the goodness in your imagination sends signals of positivity to the mind. Checking in at the end of the day helps you see your progress so you don't lose momentum. What we pay attention to expands. So when, in the evening, you check in about the good stuff that happened and write it down, you begin to see a pattern emerge as you see tangible evidence that your thoughts and intentions truly do positively influence your world. The way this actually works is through a part of the brain stem known as the reticular activating system. This area of the brain helps you focus on something that is relevant to you and tune out other stuff. It's this part of the brain that is working when, after you've decided to buy a certain kind of red car, you begin to notice that kind of car everywhere. That car has suddenly become very relevant. And so you see it. This twice-a-day check-in, via the reticular activating system, will eventually retrain your subconscious mind—and brain—and begin to reprogram it.

Breathe Deeply and Regularly

Another practice that will help calm down those stress hormones is breathing. Deeply. Through your nose. And regularly.

Try this. Take a slow, deep breath through your nose. Open up the back of your throat as you do this. Then let it out through your nose. Wait a second or two. Now take a slow, deep breath through your mouth. Exhale through your mouth. What do you notice?

The breath through your nose is much deeper because the anatomy of the nose sends the air right down to the lower lobes of the lungs where most of the blood is. Hence, a slow, deep breath through your nose is far more effective at oxygenating your lungs than a breath through the mouth. But there's more. Expanding the lower ribcage is associated with stimulating the vagus nerve as it runs through your diaphragm. This is the main nerve of the parasympathetic "rest and restore" or "rest and digest" part of the nervous system—the part that helps beat those stress hormones. There are stress receptors in the upper lobes of the lungs—the place where shallow breaths through the mouth end up, stressing you out further. On the other hand, deep breaths through your nose activate calming receptors in the lower lobes of your lungs.

Breathing through the nose also increases your body's levels of nitric oxide—a gas that is produced by the lining of every blood vessel in your body. Nitric oxide is the über-neurotransmitter that balances out all the other neurotransmitters in the body, such as serotonin, beta endorphin, and dopamine. These are the neurotransmitters that are affected by psych meds such as Prozac.

Learning how to breathe fully through our noses helps us remember who we really are while digesting excess stress hormones.

So try to take three to four slow, deep breaths through your nose multiple times a day. You can do it whenever you have a break, just to bring you back to a relaxed state. Or you can do it in the midst of a stressful event. Put sticky notes that say "BREATHE" all around your house—the bathroom mirror, the steering wheel of your car, your refrigerator door. You'll be amazed at how much healing comes from breathing deeply and regularly.

The benefits of breathing consciously through your nose are so great that I've even started to apply one of the methods developed by the late Russian doctor Konstantin Buteyko, whose groundbreaking and clinically proven work can correct asthma, snoring, sleep apnea, and other breathing conditions. Though there are many breathing exercises in the Buteyko method, the one I use is really simple. Every night, before I go to sleep, I tape my mouth shut. Sounds crazy, right? Well, here's what I've noticed. I wake up each morning with far more energy and far less grogginess than ever before. The first time you do this, you might feel a little panicky for about 15 minutes, but don't worry, your body will adjust. And then all night long you'll be in a "rest and restore" breathing pattern in which your body is metabolizing stress hormones—instead of the mouth open, snoring, "fight or flight" pattern that afflicts so many.

So remember, breathe through your nose. Breathing through your mouth actually elicits a stress response. It literally causes your body to make more stress hormones.

Move Your Body

Okay, now let's move into the body and try to calm down stress and inflammation in another way: movement. Here's the thing about movement—it is actually an incredibly powerful aid for creating and maintaining mental health. It has been found that 50 percent of mild to moderate depression can be cured simply with aerobic exercise. And not a whole lot of it either. Just 20 minutes three times per week. And walk or exercise at a pace at which you can comfortably breathe through your nose. Never exert yourself more than you can handle with nose breathing. The moment you need to breathe through your mouth, you are in "fight or flight" and the stress-hormone response will just result in cellular inflammation and, over time, depressed immunity.

One of the reasons why people don't lose weight despite loads of exercise is that they're exercising while gasping for breath with their mouths open. All this does is increase stress hormones and cellular inflammation. When you breathe slowly and steadily through your nose, you will find that your rib cage will eventually become more flexible. And you'll be able to walk and even run while breathing only through your nose. Dr. John Douillard, founder of LifeSpa in Boulder, Colorado, and author of *Body, Mind, and Sport,* has even trained people to climb Everest with no additional oxygen because of their ability to oxygenate their tissues through proper breathing during physical exertion. I know several athletes who are able to run easily, joyfully, and comfortably while breathing through their noses—something they all had to work up to. Meanwhile, those who exercise while breathing through their mouths often end up sore, stiff, tired, and dreading exercise.

Making the changes we've been talking about—setting boundaries with your vampire, working on healing wounds, and so on—is likely to lead some people to feel a bit unbounded until they get well into the process. And that's one of the reasons I recommend some basic exercise. Take a 20-minute walk three times per week. You can even do this walking up and down the hallways of a building or walking around a mall. Of course it's always best to get outside. But start where you are. The old adage "A healthy mind in a healthy body" is very true. Exercise changes the brain as much as it does your muscles.

Another thing that leads to a deterioration in the body is sitting for long periods of time. Some people have actually described sitting as the new smoking because sitting for more than six hours per day increases your risk of just about everything—from heart attack to stroke to diabetes to cancer. Even if you exercise regularly, prolonged sitting cancels out a lot of the good effects. Sitting is actually experienced by the body as a "state of weightlessness," which makes us lose our balance, our vital capacity, our bone density, our cardiac output, and many other bodily functions—just like astronauts who have been weightless in space. Joan Vernikos, Ph.D., the former director of NASA's Life Sciences Division who was responsible for keeping John Glenn healthy when he went back into space at the age of 77, says that standing every 20 to 30 minutes will make even very sedentary people in wheelchairs (those who are not paralyzed) able to get up and walk again. That is the power of moving against gravity. Because of this, I tell people that they should, at the very least, stand up and sit down every 30 minutes. For you, in your vampire-induced weakened state, this is extra important.

Many of the physical symptoms we associate with aging—pain, limited range of motion, and that shuffling walk—come from the accumulation of fascia in the body. Fascia is the network of connective tissue that connects everything in the body. It binds the skin to the muscles, encases and runs throughout all the muscles, and also connects the muscles to the bones and to every organ in the body in one continuous, uninterrupted sheath.

As we go through life, our fascia can become dense, scarred, and thickened as a result of physical, emotional, or mental stress—all of which you have endured during your vampire relationship. This stress leads to inflammation, then thickening as the tissue fibers stick together. Over time, this begins to restrict the free flow of movement and energy in the body.

The reason for restricted movement is clear—since fascia is connected throughout the body, the thickening of tissue in one place affects the fascia in every part of the body. The reason for restricted energy is a bit more complicated. Our fascia is crystalline in nature, and like any crystal, it transmits energy. This means that it can send information throughout the body very rapidly. However, when your fascia becomes dense and thickened, its ability to transmit energy decreases. Lower transmission of energy means that your "issues" get stuck in your "tissues." And your body quite literally begins to look and act old. As my intuitive friend and fascia expert Hope Matthews says, "It's not your age; it's your fascia." Happily, it's never too late to restore your fascia to a more youthful, fluid, and hydrated state.

Stretching and working this fascial tissue helps keep your body in tip-top shape. Not only are you keeping it flexible, but you are also activating acupuncture meridians that run throughout this system. These meridians are the highways along which energy flows and they are connected to every organ in your body. When you activate those meridians, you send healing energy to the organs associated with them, which is a great help as you're working to restore health after your vampire relationship.

Correct posture is another form of movement that is key to keeping fascia healthy and keeping all organs functioning healthfully. The modern-built environment tends to make us slouch and move improperly. Looking repeatedly at our cell phones with our heads down puts strain on our necks. And the end result shows up as dense fascia. There are natural, healthy postures used by athletes, children, and people in traditional societies the world over who have no back pain. It's possible to learn how to transform how you sit, stand, bend, and move in ways that are healthy. The leading authority on this is Esther Gokhale, the author of *8 Steps to a Pain-Free Back*. She teaches a system of healthy posture that helps restore your body's structural integrity.

Working your fascial meridians through specific stretching does more than help your posture and muscle tone. It also helps shore up your energetic boundaries so that you are far less susceptible to picking up other people's stuff. As I'm sure you can imagine, this helps as you work to keep energy vampires at bay. My Pilates and Intuitive Movement healer, Hope Matthews, who is also a skilled empath, told me that she no longer gets "visited" by unwanted visitors at night because she started stretching regularly. The type of stretching I'm talking about means contracting your muscles while also stretching them— exactly like a dog or cat does when they get up from sleeping—or like you do when you yawn in the morning and stretch your hands over your head. Recall that we empaths are porous. To become more like Teflon instead of Velcro, you need to move and keep your fascia healthy!

The other thing that we've seen about the fascia is that it stores emotions that haven't been processed. These emotions can then manifest as illness. The fascial information storage is how our biography becomes our biology. So when you move in new ways, you keep your fascia—and your potential—flowing. I've included a list of some of my favorite movement practices in the Resources section at the back of this book.

Clean Up Your Diet

I could write a whole book on this topic—and so could zillions of other people. There are so many different takes on this topic that I'll leave you with just a few pieces of tried-and-true advice for bringing down inflammation in your body.

The first is, eat your vegetables. No, you don't have to become a vegetarian. In fact, there are many individuals who do much better with animal protein, including red meat. But everyone needs a whole lot of vegetables. Green, leafy, and brightly colored vegetables. The more the better.

Next, keep processed, packaged foods to a minimum and eliminate all refined carbohydrates whenever possible. That includes packaged cookies, cakes, breads, rolls, and so on. Concentrate on whole foods directly from the earth or sea—unprocessed whenever possible. Organic and non-GMO if possible. When *not* possible, bless your food with Divine Love (see page 159).

And finally—and perhaps most important—avoid sugar. Sugar is an opiate that dulls pain. And if you are in a relationship with a vampire, trust me, you're in pain. Even if you don't know it intellectually. In experimental situations, when rats are given a choice between sugar water and cocaine, they go for the sugar water far more frequently. It has been estimated that sugar is eight times more addictive than heroin or other opiates. When rats are fed sugar, they can hold their paws on hot surfaces much longer. You might say that sugar is the opiate of the masses. This is why, in sitcom after sitcom, you see the characters going for ice cream or pizza or chips when under stress.

In his book *One Spirit Medicine*, anthropologist Alberto Villoldo points out that a diet that contains a lot of sugar is associated with the lower brain centers—the survival centers of the species. Whereas a diet that contains very little sugar is associated with the activation of the more evolved areas of the brain that are involved in creativity, revelation, invention, and connection with Source energy. I recall, back in the 1980s, reading research from the Tidewater Detention Home in Virginia. Sugar had been removed from the diet of these boys and aggression and violence decreased dramatically. There is no question that, in many individuals, sugar (or alcohol, which is pretty much the same thing) can trigger violent or aggressive behavior. It takes us away from our Higher Selves and keeps us stuck in a lower, slower vibration.

I know that giving up sugar may seem impossible, but you can do it. In his book *Always Hungry?* Dr. David Ludwig of Boston Children's Hospital has a 10-day introduction to his program that eliminates all sugars, including artificial sweeteners—even the healthy ones like stevia. Within 10 days, the taste buds will be reset. And an apple will taste very sweet. And so will a sweet potato. And— better yet—insulin levels will plummet, and so will the cellular inflammation that makes you feel tired, achy, and cranky. At the very least, your energy field will be boosted enough so that you'll be more "vampire resistant."

Eat Mindfully

Okay, okay. I know how hard this is. Eating on the run is sometimes the only option in your busy life. And sometimes you just want to sit in front of the TV and zone out. I get it. But eating mindfully is important. So when you're ready to eat, sit down someplace where you won't be distracted. And then chew each bite 25 times before you swallow it. If you do this, you'll find that you really, truly taste your food. When you do this for your body—and your little inner child—you'll feel truly loved and taken care of in a way that you probably weren't when you were a kid. It's a discipline, I know. But try it. You'll be amazed at how satisfying your food will be. And how much less of it you'll want to eat. And how good your digestion will be—given that digestion begins in the mouth. Eating this way will also calm down the stress hormones that so many of us empaths have floating around after interacting with vampires.

Get Your Sleep

Sleep is, hands down, the most effective way our bodies have to metabolize excess stress hormones and heal our bodies. Increasingly, research is showing how vital quality sleep is to every function in the body. Schools are finally realizing that a later start time is essential for teenagers, who need a lot of sleep, and industry is realizing how important good rest is to employee performance. When she was still at her company, The Huffington Post, Arianna Huffington, sleep activist and author of *The Sleep Revolution: Transforming Your Life One Night at a Time*, instituted nap rooms for staff. She told me that they are used regularly. I recently bought a daybed for my own office, and I am encouraging my staff to use it on those days when they simply can't keep their eyes open. While they have been socialized into thinking that the best approach is to just push through, it is most definitely *not*.

Sleep is my go-to healer, and I highly recommend it for everyone. Yes—I know there are a few rare individuals who really appear to get by on a mere four to five hours a night. They are, unfortunately, celebrated for this. For decades, those of us who have needed more sleep have felt like something is wrong with us. Medicine is a very sleep macho culture. And heaven knows, I've had more than my share of all-nighters in the emergency and delivery rooms. But this shouldn't be a way of life for anyone. When you are regularly sleep deprived, your body shifts into cellular inflammation mode. It becomes nearly impossible to lose weight, let alone live from your true authentic self.

When I've been traveling, or have had to get up earlier than my body wants to, I always schedule in a day or two when I don't have to awaken at a certain time. Instead, I just sleep as long as I want to. And sometimes that means 12 or more hours at a stretch. You read that right—12 or more hours. After all, the great apes, our closest species relative, sleep 10 hours a night. I've also heard that the great Albert Einstein routinely slept 10 hours a night.

Here are a few rules for good sleep:

- **Create an electronic "sundown":** Light from computer monitors, cell phones, and television adversely impacts melatonin levels in your brain. Melatonin, produced by the pineal gland, acts as an antioxidant and is essential for good health and sound sleep. When you fall asleep with a television screen turned on, you are bombarding your body with the wrong wavelengths for rest. Electronics are also very activating for the nervous system. No good parent puts their child to bed following a couple of hours of violent or activating television shows. Instead, there is a lovely routine in which the child goes to his or her bedroom or maybe is bathed. Then the parent reads them a story and tucks them in. This routine generally lasts about 30 minutes to an hour. We need the same love and care as that little child. I almost always take a warm bath with a cup of Epsom salts in the water before bed. The magnesium in the Epsom salts is very calming to the nervous system. I also read a little in the bathtub.

- **Sleep in the dark (if possible):** Ambient light decreases melatonin. Notice how activated you get on full moon nights when the moon is shining in your window. If necessary, get some blackout blinds—especially if you live in an area where streetlights shine in your window.

- **Get to bed by 10 P.M.:** In both Ayurvedic and traditional Chinese medicine, it is well established that the liver detox cycle in the body runs from 10 P.M. to 2 A.M. That means that your body will get maximal detox and rejuvenation time if you're sleeping during those hours instead of watching television or working on your computer.

- **Turn off your cell phone:** I know this is hard. We're addicted to the things. But having your cell phone on is bad on quite a number of levels. First of all, you leave yourself open to the texting or e-mailing whims of people who may not be so considerate of your sleep. Having your phone on also inspires you to check it first thing in the morning. I recommend that upon arising, you give yourself at least 30 minutes of introspective time before checking any e-mails or social media. Use that powerful nearly awakened clean slate to set the tone for your day. Meditate, read something inspirational, say an affirmation or two. And send Divine Love out in front of you to pave the quality of your day.

- **Consider taping your mouth shut:** As
  I mentioned earlier, taping your mouth
  shut while you sleep will train your body
  to breathe through your nose, which will
  allow your body to detox stress hormones
  far more rapidly than mouth breathing.
  Over time, this practice will actually change
  your jaw position, your rib cage, your nasal
  passages, and the quality of your sleep, not to
  mention the benefits of eliminating snoring,
  mouth breathing, and sleep apnea. I know it
  may sound crazy, but give it a try. I use 3M
  micropore paper tape, but you can use any
  hypoallergenic paper tape.

The other amazing thing about sleep is that when you sleep soundly, you tend to remember your dreams, and dreams are the way your subconscious gets your attention, which can be very handy as you're working to heal your wounds and childhood trauma. You can actually work directly with your dreams to find out what needs to be healed. So pay attention when you dream. Check in with your intuition and ask if this dream was merely an accounting of your day or if it held some deeper message. Think of your dreams as letters from your subconscious telling you what is still wounding you.

One of the most effective ways I've found to deal with wounds that come to me through dreams is to figure out what emotions are being brought up by the dream, then I feel the emotions fully, name the needs those emotions signify, and do something to get those needs met. In the example I gave earlier about the dream I had about needing to get my bags packed to catch a train—while my family completely ignored me—the emotion I woke up with in the morning was profound grief at not getting support or help. So I named those emotions, letting the grief and abandonment move through me. Then I named the needs that these emotions signified: my need for support, having my needs recognized, feeling seen, loved, and valued. Then I talked about the dream with some trusted friends so that I could immediately get support in waking time. Once I had shared my feelings and gotten support, the healing happened quite quickly.

This was a particularly dramatic dream. In many other dreams, when there is an outcome that I don't like, I just go back into the dream in waking time and rearrange the message in the dream. I create situations that meet my unmet needs. Had I done this with my dream of no one helping me, I would have gone back into the dream, asked for help, and had my entire family gather around me to help me pack my suitcase and get to the train in record time. Maybe with a nice stop for coffee first! Day dreaming and going back into the dream in waking time accesses the subconscious just the same as a dream does. And by doing this, you can quickly work with your subconscious story and upgrade it in waking life. Remember—you need never be a victim of your dreams.

Worry about the Right Things

Maintaining balance in your body has become somewhat of an obsession lately. You can see it in the vitamin section of your local grocery store and the multitude of tests your doctor orders. But there are some things you need to care about and some things you don't. And with all the stress you've experienced in your relationship, the "don't worry" part of this is very important. Here's my quick list:

Fasting insulin: This is something you should care about, and a simple test from your health-care provider can tell you where you are. Your fasting insulin level measures the amount of insulin in your bloodstream when you haven't eaten anything for at least 12 hours. Why do I tell you to check this? Because insulin levels begin to rise up to 10 years *before* most people are diagnosed with type 2 diabetes. So this test will help you keep an eye on your body's ability to process sugar—and as you remember, sugar is a huge problem for highly sensitive people who are drained of energy.

Some people may suggest that you test your fasting blood sugar, but a fasting insulin level is much more accurate. Fasting blood sugar may well remain normal for years while your pancreas is putting out too much insulin to deal with blood sugar levels that are too high.

Ideally your fasting insulin level will be below 3.

Iodine: Because of water fluoridation and chlorination, plus the addition of bromide to baked goods, far too many people have suboptimal levels of iodine in their systems. So it's good to get some additional iodine in your diet. Iodized salt is the source that most people think of when they think about how to get more iodine; however, this salt comes with other problems. For saltiness, I generally recommend sea salt and Himalayan pink, but they don't contain iodine. So how do you get iodine and avoid the problems? You eat sea vegetables, take kelp tablets, or simply put drops of Lugol's solution in water. Generally seven drops of 2 percent Lugol's in water will be sufficient. Start very slowly if you are on thyroid medication, and if possible, work with a health-care practitioner who knows how to monitor your thyroid status.

Iodine is absolutely essential for optimal thyroid, ovary, and breast health. Very often women with sore breasts will have complete relief after adding iodine to their diets. Note that when you start taking iodine, you may well get a rash or other detox reaction as the iodine allows the excess chlorine, fluoride, and bromide to leave the body. People mistake this for being allergic to iodine.

Other minerals: Because of the soil depletion, most of us need more minerals in our diet. Minerals—especially magnesium—are what hold the electromagnetic charge of our biological fields. When minerals are depleted, we become like a sluggish computer that boots really slowly. The most effective sources of these minerals I've ever found are Dr. Carolyn Dean's ReMag and ReMyte liquid magnesium and other minerals. Dr. Dean wrote *The Magnesium Miracle* and her research on the subject is the most accurate I've ever found. If you have leg cramps, atrial fibrillation, difficulty sleeping, headaches, or anxiety—all could be signs of magnesium deficiency. Taking magnesium in this form allows you to achieve a much higher dose without the usual bowel side effects of oral magnesium, which often causes loose stools. I add one teaspoon each of ReMag and ReMyte to a pint of water to which some Himalayan salt has been added. I make up the water ahead of time—putting one teaspoon of Himalayan salt in a gallon of water. I then keep this at room temperature in the kitchen so it's ready each morning. The ReMag and ReMyte don't taste good. So I just add two tablespoons of Bragg's organic apple cider vinegar to the mix.

Vitamin D: Get your vitamin D checked. An optimal level of vitamin D is between 40 and 60 pg/mL (picograms per millileter). Those with optimal vitamin D levels have half the risk of multiple sclerosis, heart disease, breast cancer, and bowel cancer.

You can get plenty of vitamin D through regular exposure to sunlight. Thirty minutes of sun exposure—if you are fair skinned—over most of your body will give you 10,000 IU (international units) of this vitamin, all made under the skin. If you are darker skinned, you'll need to stay out in the sun longer to get the same amount of vitamin D. Dark-skinned people can still get sunburned, so everyone needs to start slowly and build up. For those of us in the northern hemisphere, that's 5–10 minutes a day starting at the end of March and building up to 30–60 minutes over as much of your body as possible in mid-morning or late afternoon as the summer progresses. Note that after mid-October, you don't really get enough of the UVB (shortwave ultraviolet) rays in the north to make vitamin D under the skin. So during the fall, winter, and early spring (and when you can't get outside in the summer), supplement with 5,000 IU of vitamin D per day.

Natural light is a nutrient as well. When you walk in ambient natural light, you are actually nourishing your brain and balancing your hormones via the retina of the eye.

Cholesterol: This is one area where I vary a bit from the medical establishment. Cholesterol has been made squarely into an enemy over the past few decades, and in my opinion, this has done far more harm than good. Most people needn't worry about cholesterol until it's nearly 300. Many people in their 90s who are perfectly healthy have cholesterols of 260 to 300. There are far too many people taking statin drugs, which are associated with memory loss, muscle pain, and breast cancer. So while I suggest you get your cholesterol tested, don't just accept your doctor's prescription. Do your own research and then decide.

Become Vaccine Savvy

Starting in 1991, the recommended childhood vaccine schedule from the CDC (Centers for Disease Control and Prevention) tripled the number of shots it listed. And at the same time, Congress granted vaccine manufacturers full immunity from any lawsuits resulting from vaccine injuries. Since that time, the number of recommended adult vaccines has also increased dramatically. Once you understand the history and politics of vaccines, you will quickly see that there is a much more complicated story here. Besides, it is not infectious diseases that are killing so many people now. It's chronic degenerative diseases.

Carefully consider whether or not to get "routine" vaccines such as shingles, flu, and pneumonia. All vaccines contain a plethora of toxic substances that can adversely affect health, especially in those as sensitive as empaths. Vaccines are neither universally safe nor effective. For an eye-opening and scientifically rigorous look at vaccines, I highly recommend that you read Dr. Suzanne Humphries's book *Dissolving Illusions: Disease, Vaccines, and the Forgotten History*. Dr. Humphries is a board-certified internist and nephrologist whose eyes were opened to the risks associated with vaccines when her dialysis patients experienced deteriorating renal function after their routine vaccines at the hospital. Remember, you're an empath. You know things. And one of those things is how to heal and be healthy—despite everything you've been programmed to believe.

Let Mother Earth Heal You

Back in the days before antibiotics, people with tuberculosis were sent to sanitariums where they spent time every day lying out in the sun and also exercising in the fresh air. Many were cured completely this way. But we've forgotten about this in the era of antibiotics, which is now coming to an end as overuse of antibiotics has created superbugs of all kinds that are antibiotic-resistant.

Just 20 minutes of standing barefoot on Mother Earth has been shown to decrease cellular inflammation by 20 percent. When you're jet-lagged, standing barefoot on the ground will rejuvenate you quickly. That's because the Earth herself emits negatively charged electrons that feel really good and are very healthy. If you can't take off your shoes, then hold on to a tree. That too will ground you and your energy. Too much screen time—in front of cell phones and computers—is associated with all kinds of adverse effects on our electromagnetic systems. But this can be counteracted with regular time just standing on the ground.

KNOW YOURSELF

There are endless books on what to eat and when. How to exercise. How to meditate. So here's my last piece of advice. Before choosing a path, do this: Sit down. Take a slow, deep breath through your nose. Now exhale slowly through your nose. Repeat that breath. Breathe in and out through your nose a third time. You have now lowered your stress hormone levels by activating your parasympathetic nervous system. So now you're ready for some self-inquiry. Ask yourself, "How can I best preserve my life energy and love myself and my body right now?" Write down your answer. It will be right there. Whispering in your ear.

Chapter 11

STANDING AS THE LIGHT YOU ARE

If you've made it this far in this book, I hope you've been doing the necessary work to heal your mind, your emotions, and your body. But there is one final step in healing—a step that will help you regain or maintain good health emotionally and physically. Most important, truly embodying this step will render you virtually vampire-proof. It is the most exhilarating and liberating thing I've ever discovered. The final step is remembering to stand as the light you are—something that will lead to a life in which you are living as your highest and most fulfilled version of yourself. And when you do this, you are inoculated from the Darkness around you.

YOU ARE THE LIGHT

If there's anything I hope you've learned from reading this book, it's that you are special. There's a reason you fall prey to energy vampires. There's a reason you work so hard to help other people. There's a reason you are the person people turn to in tough situations. The reason is that you are a Lightworker. You are here to anchor light and well-being for the entire planet. You are here to emit high-frequency healing energy. And until you stand as the light you are, you will not feel complete. You will not move to the higher states of love and joy that keep you protected from the people who feed off your energy.

The light of empaths and old-soul empaths emanates from our intent. Our intent is reaching a hand out to the Divine—to God. And whenever we do this, we anchor in more light. And emit more light and healing as a result. Remember what I said in the beginning of this book. Our intent, our light, is always grounded in love, compassion, and service, not self-sacrifice and martyrdom. Self-sacrifice and martyrdom have been tools of Darkness used by Darkness in the old energy. They are the tools of enslavement. When you give away your power or focus on trying to fix the unfixable, you dim your light. And that is one of the lessons you came to learn. This is why vampires can be such profound teachers.

When you love yourself first, you stand as the light. When you forgive yourself for any real or imagined "sins," you stand as the light. When you stop perpetuating the myth that you are flawed and that something is wrong with you, you stand as the light. When you fill up your self-love bank account, you stand as the light. And when you humbly acknowledge your greatness with humility, you stand as the light.

Whenever you feel guilt or shame or humiliation, you can get through it using the techniques and understandings you've learned in this book. And the moment you do that, you are clearing that particular vibration from the entire collective.

Everything you do for yourself makes it safer for others to do better for themselves. Everything you do for you, you're doing for the whole—for the place where we are all connected. When you do this, it radiates an energy from you that tells people it's safe for them to feel all of what they feel as well. It also shows vampires that you are not available to be their prey.

The amazing thing about empaths is that our energy field changes things. It illuminates the darkness and helps clear it. This is what it means to be a Lightworker. We are here to feel and clear dark emotions from the collective, and speed up the return of loving-kindness to the planet. Every time we feel pain, sorrow, guilt, or longing, it is not just ours. We are actually feeling and clearing that particular kind of pain or sorrow for everyone. This is the profound service for which we were born. It isn't even conscious. It's just the way it is. We didn't know that as children. Now we do. Our light illuminates whatever place we find ourselves. And the things that have hidden in the dark suddenly become visible—the vampires and their tactics no longer affect us or the people around us.

Spiritual teacher Dolores Cannon, in her book *The Three Waves of Volunteers and the New Earth*, speaks of three types of people who have come to earth to change the energy of the planet so we can avoid a terrible disaster. The old-soul empaths seem to fall into the second wave of these people. They are "antennas, beacons, generators, channels of energy. They have come in with a unique energy that greatly affects others. They don't have to *do* anything. They just have to *be*. I have been told that just by walking through a crowded mall or grocery store their energy affects everyone they come in contact with. It is that strong, and of course, they do not realize this consciously. The paradox is that although they are supposed to be affecting people by their energy, they really don't feel comfortable being around people. So many of them stay home secluded, to avoid mixing with others; even working from their homes. Thus they are defeating their purpose."

THE DARKNESS

Now here's the thing. There is darkness in the world, but there is also darkness in you. It's in each and every one of us, and we can choose the Darkness or we can choose the light. And you can get as light as you want, or as dark as you want. It's all your choice. I remember reading a section in Paulo Coelho's book *Eleven Minutes* about a woman from Brazil who had been invited to Switzerland for what she thought was a better job and a better life. When she arrived, she found herself working in a brothel. While most of her clients were the type you would expect at a brothel, there was one man who just wanted to talk. He turned out to be a very astute spiritual advisor for her. When one of her clients requested sadomasochistic practices, her mentor warned her against starting down that road of combining sexual energy with humiliation, pain, and shame. Because there would be no end to how far down she could go. It would simply get darker and darker and deeper and deeper. It would require more and more of her energy. It is the same with anything we do. We can run for the Darkness or we can run for the light.

That dark part of you is the part that's saying, "I don't believe all this nonsense. There's nothing special about me. I've just had some bad luck." Or "greed and every man for himself are just part of human nature. It will always be a dog-eat-dog planet." The Darkness sponsors unbelief. It knows that if a skeptic looks, they'll see something that makes the Darkness obsolete. So the dark does everything in its power to keep you from looking. This is why so many people do not awaken to their light. Instead they make fun of spiritual pursuits—calling them hogwash. Fairy talk? Angels? Prayer? You've got to be kidding me. When I was in medical school, a colleague said to me, "I can't believe you're reading a book about angels. A woman of your intelligence. Come ON." Believing in past lives, energy fields, flower essences, and things that are beyond the realm of Newtonian physics? These are myths that clear-thinking adults dismiss out of hand. But this is precisely where you can find the light. When you reject the intangible, you decrease your access to the light, and that's when the dark sits on you.

Our society has been built on darkness. Authority figures pit people against each other to keep wars going. Corporations look out for profits above all else because money is held up as the pinnacle of success. Schools instill fear and stress because there is nothing worse than falling short of societal expectations. With these pressures and the 24/7 bad news, it's easy to fall into despair and pessimism, which in turn makes it more likely that you'll sink into greed, manipulation, or addiction. Anything to numb the pain. But you falling into despair or buying into the ability of darkness to ameliorate your suffering is where Darkness gets its power.

The choice you need to make is to open the door to the light.

The dark thing inside you will be with you as long as you're on earth. Darkness has free reign until you begin to question things spiritually. When you ask, "Who am I?" the light begins to come in. You begin to have control over the Darkness through your choices and your thoughts. Remember this. You are more powerful than any dark thing on this planet. Once you decide to step into the light, the Darkness will lose its grip on you. And your life will take a turn for the better.

But for this to happen, you have to choose to step out of fear. You cannot allow yourself to be scared to death or worried sick. Notice those terms. They are phrases that illustrate the power of fear and worry.

Fear immobilizes you. It's the dark part of you that says, "I cannot get ahead." "I'm too old." "It's normal to get sick as you get older." "It's too late for me." "I can't change this." All the negatives. That's how fear and darkness work. When you let these in, you let in the darkness of the vampires around you.

Fear starts in the gut. It is a lower-vibration attribute of humanity that can be used to manipulate people. It pretty much drives conventional medicine. If you don't get this test, you could die. If you don't take this medicine, you could die. If you don't learn how to control fear, it will invade your mind and begin to run your life.

So you must stop fear in its tracks. I know this sounds simplistic, but stopping fear begins with simply noticing it—shining a light on it. Next time you have a fearful response say, "Stop. I know what you're doing. STOP." Then congratulate yourself for your skill of noticing your fear and stopping it. It really can be that simple. Just remember that fear is food for Darkness. We are not meant to walk in fear. I know what you're thinking: *I've tried this before—the affirmations, the positive stuff. It just doesn't work.* That's no longer true in the new energy—the energy that shifted in 2012. Things are different now.

You have immense amounts of wisdom, so let your wisdom dissipate your fear. As Elizabeth Gilbert says in her book *Big Magic*, fear will always be with us. It's not going away. But it doesn't have to drive the car. You can put it in the backseat. And not let it choose the radio station. I wouldn't buckle its seat belt either if I were you. No need making it feel more secure.

When you give in to your fear, your anger, or your sadness, you are fueling the Darkness and giving power to the vampires.

If all you do is strike one match—light one light—and say, "Dear God . . . show me. Show me." Just say, "I'm ready to know. Show me what I'm meant to do. I'm ready to listen." Don't be surprised if love flows into your heart. If angels take your hands and vampires retreat.

Life on earth is not supposed to be miserable. Our purpose should be to bring as much Spirit (or God) as possible right down into the density of matter. Our goal should be to bring heaven right down to earth. And we can do that because God resides within each of us. That's right—a little piece of God is within you. That is the big secret—and the key to liberation. The phrase "To thine own self be true" speaks to this ever-present guidance.

Every culture that has ever been on earth has asked the question: "Who am I? Why am I here?"

Every inspired scripture that has ever been written was written by a human being who was in touch with the God within. Do you think that God—our Creator—has stopped talking to us?

You can begin a dialogue with the God within any time you want. Ask and it is given.

The thing is that each of us is an individual. The God that comes through you will be different from the God that comes through me. There aren't any rules and regulations written on any tablets. But your Divinity is written in your DNA the minute you rise to the occasion of being the light.

One of the most provocative things that Jesus said was "These things and more, you shall do also." And what he meant by that is that we too have the same power that he did. In my view, that is the second coming. When we realize the power we have had in our hearts, minds, and bodies all along.

When you move past fear and victimhood, there is no stopping how bright your light can shine. Louise Hay, the founder of Hay House, the company that published this book, is a brilliant example of this. Louise grew up in poverty with a stepfather who beat and sexually abused her. She put a child up for adoption and never saw that child again. She developed cervical cancer in her early 20s but she learned how to heal it with dietary change and affirmations. After marrying the man of her dreams, she was devastated when he asked for a divorce. But she didn't give in to her despair. She moved forward, and later in life even felt grateful for him, saying, "He made me Louise Hay." She self-published a book called *You Can Heal Your Life* when she was nearly 60. The book became a number-one *New York Times* bestseller the same week she appeared on the *Phil Donahue* and *Oprah Winfrey* television shows. And thus Hay House was born.

Hay House operates a network of light throughout the world. All because one woman decided to transform her considerable darkness into light. A light that keeps on growing and growing with each passing year. That is the power of the human being as creator.

Louise is just one of many examples, but now is the time for each of us to grab hold of our personal power. The world is shifting. In fact, so much light is streaming onto planet Earth right now—the darkness is very apparent. The darkness has always been here, but now it's right out there for everyone to see. But the light is getting so very bright. Robert Fritchie, who has studied with the late Marcel Vogel and worked with Divine Love for 25 years, says that the energy we call Divine Love has stabilized on the planet ever since 2012. And so what used to take the healing power of five people can be accomplished now by just one.

Make no mistake, the Darkness is strong and it dies hard. It is pulling out all the stops. And that is why, despite everything you've been told, the more willing you are to love yourself and be the light that you are—which includes radiating joy and optimism—the faster the Darkness will go away. The Darkness and its vampire minions are fighting for their lives. But they know that the jig is up. One person who is light positively affects 10,000 who are in Darkness. It's time to take up the banner of Lightworker.

THE PRACTICALITIES OF STANDING AS THE LIGHT

So what does this all mean in a practical sense?

It means that it's not your job to suffer and take crap from vampires—of any sort. You are here to transform darkness into light, so the next time someone pulls at your heart strings—but never, ever does anything for themselves other than feed off your goodwill—tell them to go away. Investigate before automatically assuming that they are well-meaning. This is especially true if they are charismatic or good-looking and at first you feel flattered by their attention. Remember this phrase: "You haven't been chosen. You've been targeted." Then laugh.

The next time someone is mean or critical, just know that it is your job to clean that up within you. It is not your job to try to change them. Nor is it your job to seek out the darkness and try to illuminate it with your will. You just have to deal with what's right in front of you.

If someone is rude or mean to you, just say "Thank you." And then, either to yourself or to them, say, "I'm sorry for your pain. Bless you." You might even do it with the same force as "F**K you." But it's "BLESS you" instead.

Standing as the light—and protecting yourself from vampires and the darkness—means putting yourself first. Earlier this week, I got an e-mail about an organic farm in Oregon that was about to be sprayed with a deadly herbicide because the county interpreted a statute that suggested that the weeds on the farm were dangerous. As a result, this certified organic farm was in danger of being decimated. This is going on all over the place. All the time. And if you, like me, tend toward taking action, I'll bet your in-box is full of this kind of thing.

But this time, instead of writing to the county commissioner of this town in Oregon—which is all the way across the country—I stopped myself. Yes. I want to save everyone. That's my nature, but I had to realize that this wasn't my fight. I have plenty of things that grab my attention right here in my own little town. Like the zoning laws. And how to keep our farmland from being sold for development. And how to keep our local river clean and free of pollutants. All of those things and more are right here in front of my face. I can talk with my neighbors about them. And do something. To stand as a powerful Lightworker, I couldn't deplete my energy working for a faraway cause. I needed to focus my light on my community.

Kind of like my friend Carolyn, who lives on the Hudson River. When she saw a whole bunch of oil barges parked out in front of her house and discovered that these barges were being used to export tar sands oil out of the country, which could wreak havoc on the environment, she got to work. She passionately and skillfully brought all her neighbors together—and eventually many of the towns all up and down the Hudson—to protest the potential environmental devastation to her beloved river. This is love in action. She is a force of light with what is right in front of her.

And I suggest you do the same.

Deal with what is right in front of you. Not with what you see on the news, which is highly manipulated and designed to keep you fearful and angry. Remember that 70 percent of what you see on mainstream television is brought to you by the pharmaceutical industry. They have a vested interest in keeping you numb and drugged. Literally.

FOR OR AGAINST

As you work to focus your light, there are other things you can do to protect yourself. The first is to fight *for* something, rather than *against* something. Whenever you are anti something, you are giving power to what you don't want. When you are protesting something, you are joining with a community in a state of uprising and fighting. This makes it very easy for the arrogant powers that be (the few who've been controlling the many through fear and manipulation) to see you as a kind of social criminal. You don't get much unseen help this way.

In order for you to access your full power as a creative human being, you have to be *for* something. When you come together in a community of consciousness for something, then you are an announcer of well-being. The community is spiritually fed. Everyone is respected. Everyone has a chance to win and to feel success. While my friend Carolyn and her group protested, they protested in favor of something. They joined together to preserve the beautiful habitat of the Hudson River Valley and surrounding communities.

Empaths are not meant to fight. We don't have the nervous systems for it. We're too sensitive. Only those with huge egos have the kind of stamina that it takes to fight on and on and on. Instead, it is our job to decide what causes truly move our hearts. And then participate only to the extent that that participation feeds us in some way. Remember—martyrdom and self-sacrifice are not sustainable. And though they are well-worn paths for empaths, please guard against them.

When something comes into your environment that doesn't support the idea that all is well, then don't participate. Tell the God within that this is not a show you want to watch. Remember, you are standing for the light. And when you do that, you become very attractive to other people of light—not to energy vampires.

The other thing we need to do is to see the light as it is and push it out.

Hollywood has glamorized the spiritual experience, so we're all waiting for choirs of angels or puffs of purple smoke. But in truth, connecting with the light that you are is often far more subtle. As Scottish angel communicator Kyle Gray says, "What we need has already been given. The angels are here now. Most of time we are not. But when we say thank you, we choose to arrive at the same place the angels are." And when we literally feel ourselves pushing out the light that we are, we are protected. Always. You can no longer be affected by the Darkness and its cohorts.

The increase in the light on the planet is affecting your DNA, and that means that we can now live longer than we've been told we can. As long as you remember the light that you are and connect with Divine Love often. And stop buying into ageism in all its forms.

Stop giving all the credit to some God outside of you. Instead, go within. Meditate. Pray. Connect often. Begin to look for the shift that is now taking place on the planet. Philosopher Rob Brezsny has coined a good word and written a book by the same title: *Pronoia*—the belief that the universe is conspiring for your good. Here's the thing. The more you look for what's good, the more of it you will see. And the more the darkness will run the other way.

Believe it or not, we are living in the safest time on earth. There are fewer wars than ever before. Instead we have more news outlets that need to fill airtime with bad news in order to keep viewers locked in. Turn them off. Consume mainstream news sparingly. And with a well-schooled eye as to who is funding it.

Notice what's working on the planet. For example, in the French documentary *Demain* (*Tomorrow*), the filmmakers traveled all over the globe and found that communities worldwide are often solving their own problems brilliantly—without complex government control. An example? San Francisco has an 80 percent recycling rate. And there are farmers producing enough food on small acreage to feed their entire communities. One of my favorite success stories is documented in a movie called *One Hundred Thousand Beating Hearts,* in which a former good ol' boy factory farmer has saved his Georgia community by switching to sustainable, organic farming practice. He wisely says that he's not here to save the world. He's just here to tend to the beings on his farm.

THE DIVINITY INSIDE YOU

Earlier this year I went to the final concert of the season for the Portland Symphony Orchestra. The guest artist for the Bruch *Violin Concerto No. 1 in G minor* was a young man by the name of Alexi Kenney. And when he started to play, I was transfixed. I had never heard a violin played like that before. It was as though Alexi was being used as a Divine channel, as though he were put on earth to make the violin sound like that so that the air around him— and throughout the auditorium—healed all of us. The audience was equally transfixed. When he finished, we all rose as one, cheering with appreciation as he took several curtain calls. And then played us an incredible Piazzolla encore which you can see on YouTube. For me, this was an experience of God—coming right through Alexi's violin. My body is a tuning fork for this sort of thing. It's how I access Divinity. Your body is the same. You just have to find the right vibration. Identify what lights you up. And when you find it, notice it. Feel it. Expand on it. Talk about it. Take the ride. Don't get trapped in your intellect.

And finally, watch for the changes that are happening all around. That you'll never see in the mainstream media.

I strongly believe that in the next decade we are going to see new kinds of leaders. Integrity is going to come roaring back. In business, in politics, in families. I already see it happening. Our leaders will be here to serve the collective, not rob it or dupe it. And the rising consciousness of humanity will no longer be swayed by vicious, negative campaigning. We will have had enough. And slowly, ever so slowly, that edge that vampires have had for centuries will go away. We will be living our lives as whole beings, from the inside out. We will know Darkness when we see it and feel it . . . and we will no longer feed it on any level.

Watch for governments to change. The first that does it will be a breath of fresh air. Others will follow. Businesses will compete with each other for who has the most integrity. The zero-sum model (there's only so much to go around so I win, you lose) will be replaced by nature's model. There's enough for everyone.

When you see it in that arena, you'll know that it's real.

As we stand as the light that we are and no longer give our power away to vampires of all stripes, we create a standing wave—a grid of light. A grid that connects us all over the world. And makes it easier and easier to trust ourselves. And what we know and feel. We find our real tribes. We no longer feel alone.

Together all we have to do is gently press on the door of a new reality. And get down on our knees in thanks.

RESOURCES

In this section, I'm compiling a great number of resources—from books to videos to websites—to help you on your journey to recovery. These will guide you as you search for more information about everything from recognizing vampires to finding your preferred method of healthy movement.

RECOGNIZING/RECOVERING FROM VAMPIRE ABUSE

Books

- *Character Disturbance: The Phenomenon of Our Age*, by George K. Simon, Jr., Ph.D.

- *How Did We End Up Here?: Surviving and Thriving in a Character-Disordered World*, by George K. Simon, Jr., Ph.D.

- *How to Spot a Dangerous Man before You Get Involved*, by Sandra L. Brown, M.A.

- *In Sheep's Clothing: Understanding and Dealing with Manipulative People*, by George K. Simon, Jr., Ph.D.

- *Outwitting the Devil: The Secret to Freedom and Success*, by Napoleon Hill

- *Snakes in Suits: When Psychopaths Go to Work*, by Paul Babiak, Ph.D., and Robert D. Hare, Ph.D.

- *The Sociopath Next Door*, by Martha Stout, Ph.D.

- *Stop Walking on Eggshells: Taking Your Life Back When Someone You Care About Has Borderline Personality Disorder*, by Paul T. Mason, M.S., and Randi Kreger

- *Without Conscience: The Disturbing World of the Psychopaths Among Us*, by Robert D. Hare, Ph.D.

- *Women Who Love Psychopaths: Inside the Relationships of Inevitable Harm with Psychopaths, Sociopaths & Narcissists*, by Sandra L. Brown, M.A.

Documentaries and Illuminating Television Shows

- *Big Little Lies*, a seven-part miniseries that showcases the way in which a psychopath affects his family

- *Doctor Foster*, a beautifully done drama about a physician and her vampire husband—and how she woke up and took back her power

- *Enron: The Smartest Guys in the Room*, directed by Alex Gibney
- *Going Clear: Scientology and the Prison of Belief*, directed by Alex Gibney

Online Resources

- George K. Simon, Jr., Ph.D. (drgeorgesimon. com): Psychologist George Simon is a leading expert on manipulators and other disturbed characters. His website has a great deal of information on character disorders. His YouTube channel also features informative videos on this topic: youtube.com/user/ georgeksimon/videos.

- Judith Orloff, M.D. (drjudithorloff.com): Psychiatrist and best-selling author of *The Empath's Survival Guide,* Dr. Judith Orloff offers an online support group for empaths. You can find Dr. Orloff's Empath Support Community at facebook.com/ groups/929510143757438.

- Melanie Tonia Evans (melanietoniaevans. com): Melanie is an expert is narcissistic abuse recovery. On her website, she has healing programs for purchase. Once you join the Narcissistic Abuse Recovery Program, you also have access to a worldwide online support group and an online course for recovery from narcissistic abuse. You can also tune in to her YouTube channel, ThriverTV (youtube.com/user/MelanieToniaEvans).

- Sandra L. Brown, M.A. (saferelationshipsmagazine.com): Sandra Brown is the founder of the Institute for Relational Harm Reduction and Public Pathology Education, which focuses on helping people heal from pathological love relationships. The Institute has both tele-counseling, low-cost online programs, and retreats that will help you on your pathway to recovery. Sandra also has a series of YouTube video interviews that are excellent. Just google the following and you'll find them: YouTube Sandra Brown Women Who Love Psychopaths. She also has a Relational Harm Reduction show on blogtalk radio (blogtalkradio.com/relational-harm-reduction). Finally, she has a set of wonderful columns on pathological relationships on *Psychology Today* online (psychologytoday.com/blog/pathological-relationships).

- Shrink4Men (shrink4men.com): A website to support men who have been in abusive relationships in which women are the perpetrators.

- Sil Reynolds, R.N., F.N.P. (motheringanddaughtering.com): Sil is a nurse practitioner, psychotherapist, and mothering coach with more than 30 years of experience helping women create joyful, balanced, and meaningful lives. She is the co-author, with her daughter, Eliza·Reynolds, of *Mothering & Daughtering: Keeping Your Bond Strong Through the Teen Years*. She assists women—especially mothers—in healing from the aftermath of a pathological love relationship.

- Survivor Treatment (survivortreatment.com): An organization of professionals trained in the treatment of people who have been or are in relationships with vampires. The counselors know how to deal with all aspects of personality disorder in order to provide proper treatment. They also have a group for therapists on LinkedIn (linkedin.com/groups/12016965).

ANTI-INFLAMMATORY DIET

- "11 Food Rules for the Ultimate Anti-Inflammatory Diet," by Dr. Gary Kaplan (mindbodygreen.com/0-22607/11-food-rules-for-the-ultimate-anti-inflammatory-diet.html)

- *Always Hungry?: Conquer Cravings, Retrain Your Fat Cells & Lose Weight Permanently*, by David Ludwig, M.D., Ph.D.

- *The Anti-Inflammatory Diet & Action Plans: 4-Week Meal Plans to Heal the Immune System and Restore Overall Health*, by Dorothy Calimeris and Sondi Bruner

- *Cultured Food in a Jar: 100+ Probiotic Recipes to Inspire and Change Your Life*, by Donna Schwenk

- *The Immune System Recovery Plan: A Doctor's 4-Step Program to Treat Autoimmune Disease*, by Susan Blum, M.D., M.P.H.

- *Colorado Cleanse 4.0: 14-Day Ayurvedic Digestive Detox and Lymph Cleanse with Seasonal Cookbook*, by Dr. John Douillard

- *Medical Medium Life-Changing Foods: Save Yourself and the Ones You Love with the Hidden Healing Powers of Fruits & Vegetables*, by Anthony William

- *Medical Medium Thyroid Healing: The Truth Behind Hashimoto's, Graves', Insomnia, Hypothyroidism, Thyroid Nodules & Epstein-Barr*, by Anthony William

- *The Obesity Code: Unlocking the Secrets of Weight Loss*, by Jason Fung, M.D.

BREATHING

- Buteyko Clinic International, buteykoclinic.com

- *Close Your Mouth: Buteyko Breathing Clinic Self-Help Manual*, by Patrick McKeown

EMOTIONAL/WOUND HEALING

- Matt Kahn: *Whatever Arises, Love That: A Love Revolution That Begins with You*; youtube.com/user/JulieMuse

- *The MindBody Code: How to Change the Beliefs that Limit Your Health, Longevity, and Success*, by Dr. Mario Martinez

- Robert G. Fritchie, World Service Institute and the Divine Love healing process, worldserviceinstitute.org; *Being at One with the Divine: Self-Healing with Divine Love*; *Divine Love Self Healing: The At Oneness Healing System*

- Divine Love Healing Process webinar (free): worldserviceinstitute.org

- *Repetition: Past Lives, Life, and Rebirth*, by Doris Eliana Cohen, Ph.D.

FEAR/EMPOWERMENT

- *Big Magic: Creative Living Beyond Fear*, by Elizabeth Gilbert

- Brené Brown (brenebrown.com): *Daring Greatly: How the Courage to Be Vulnerable Transforms the Way We Live, Love, Parent, and Lead*; *The Gifts of Imperfection: Let Go of Who You Think You're Supposed to Be and Embrace Who You Are*

- Dr. Mario Martinez (biocognitive.com): Dr. Martinez works via Skype with individuals from all over the world, assisting with everything from weight loss and addiction to personal empowerment.

HEALTHY MOVEMENT

- *Body, Mind, and Sport: The Mind-Body Guide to Lifelong Health, Fitness, and Your Personal Best,* by John Douillard

- The Center for Intuitive Movement Healing, with Hope Matthews and Chris Renfrow, thecenterforintuitivemovementhealing.com

- Clear Passage, clearpassage.com, specializing in fascial release for surgical adhesions, bowel obstruction, and infertility

- *Designed to Move: The Science-Backed Program to Fight Sitting Disease and Enjoy Lifelong Health,* by Joan Vernikos, Ph.D.

- Esther Gokhale: Gokhale Method (gokhalemethod.com); *8 Steps to a Pain-Free Back*

- John F. Barnes's Myofascial Release Approach, myofascialrelease.com

- Katy Bowman, M.S., Nutritious Movement (nutritiousmovement.com): Katy Says podcast; *Move Your DNA: Restore Your Health through Natural Movement*

- Rodney Yee, yeeyoga.com

- *Sitting Kills, Moving Heals: How Everyday Movement Will Prevent Pain, Illness, and Early Death—and Exercise Alone Won't,* by Joan Vernikos, Ph.D.

STRESS REDUCTION

- *Full Catastrophe Living (Revised Edition): Using the Wisdom of Your Body and Mind to Face Stress, Pain, and Illness*, by Jon Kabat- Zinn

- Nick Ortner (thetappingsolution.com): *The Tapping Solution: A Revolutionary System for Stress-Free Living*

STANDING AS THE LIGHT YOU ARE

- Esther Hicks (abraham-hicks.com): *Ask and It Is Given: Learning to Manifest Your Desires*

- Lee Carroll (kryon.com): Lee Carroll has many uplifting and informative YouTube videos that I highly recommend for old-soul empaths. He also lectures worldwide.

- Louise Hay (louisehay.com; healyourlife.com): *You Can Heal Your Life*

REFERENCES

I am forever grateful for the interviews I was able to do with experts in fields associated with the material in this book. Being able to turn to knowledgeable people, such as Sandra Brown, George Simon, Mario Martinez, and a host of others, was invaluable, as were the many written resources I was able to access. Below is a list of many of the books and articles that were used in the creation of this book.

American Psychological Association, *Stress in America: Our Health at Risk* (2012): www.apa.org/news/press/releases/stress/2011/final-2011.pdf.

Bradley Hagerty, Barbara, "When Your Child Is a Psychopath," *The Atlantic* (June 2017): www.theatlantic.com/magazine/archive/2017/06/when-your-child-is-a-psychopath/524502.

Brezsny, Rob, *Pronoia Is the Antidote for Paranoia, Revised and Expanded: How the Whole World Is Conspiring to Shower You with Blessings* (Berkeley, CA: North Atlantic Books, 2009).

Brown, Sandra L., *How to Spot a Dangerous Man Before You Get Involved* (Alameda, CA: Hunter House Publishers, 2005).

———, *Women Who Love Psychopaths: Inside the Relationships of Inevitable Harm with Psychopaths, Sociopaths & Narcissists,* Third Edition (Hilton Head, SC: Mask Publishing, 2018).

Cannon, Dolores, *The Three Waves of Volunteers & the New Earth* (Huntsville, AR: Ozark Mountain Publishing, Inc., 2011).

Carroll, Lee, *Alchemy of the Human Spirit: A Guide to Transition into the New Age (Kryon Book Three)* (San Diego, CA: The Kryon Writings, Inc., 1995).

———, *Partnering with God: Practical Information for the New Millennium (Kryon Book Six)* (San Diego, CA: The Kryon Writings, Inc., 2002).

———, *The Recalibration of Humanity: 2013 and Beyond* (San Diego, CA: The Kryon Writings, Inc., 2013).

Cohen, Doris, *Repetition: Past Lives, Life, and Rebirth* (Carlsbad, CA: Hay House, Inc., 2008).

Colosio, Marco et al, "Neural Mechanisms of Cognitive Dissonance (Revised): An EEG Study," *The Journal of Neuroscience* 24 (April 2017): 3209–16: doi.org/10.1523/JNEUROSCI.3209-16.2017.

Decety, Jean et al, "An fMRI Study of Affective Perspective-Taking in Individuals with Psychopathy: Imagining Another in Pain Does Not Evoke Empathy," *Frontiers of Human Neuroscience* (Sept 24, 2013): doi.org/10.3389/fnhum.2013.00489.

Diagnostic and Statistical Manual of Mental Disorders, 5th Edition, American Psychiatric Publishing (May 2013).

Festinger, Leon, *A Theory of Cognitive Dissonance* (Stanford, CA: Stanford University Press, 1957).

Gilbert, Elizabeth, *Big Magic: Creative Living Beyond Fear* (New York: Riverhead Books, 2015).

Hare, Robert D., *Without Conscience: The Disturbing World of the Psychopaths Among Us* (New York: The Guilford Press, 1999).

Hendricks, Gay, *The Big Leap: Conquer Your Hidden Fear and Take Life to the Next Level* (New York: HarperOne, 2010).

Huffington, Ariana, *The Sleep Revolution: Transforming Your Life, One Night at a Time* (New York: Harmony Books, 2016).

Kahn, Matt, *Whatever Arises, Love That: A Love Revolution That Begins with You* (Boulder, CO: Sounds True, 2016).

Lipton, Bruce, *The Biology of Belief: Unleashing the Power of Consciousness, Matter & Miracles* (Carlsbad, CA: Hay House, Inc., 2006).

Ludwig, David, *Always Hungry?: Conquer Cravings, Retrain Your Fat Cells, and Lose Weight Permanently* (New York: Grand Central Life & Style, 2016).

Martinez, Mario, "Fibromyalgia: The Learning of an Illness and Its PNI Correlates": www.academia.edu/8794606/Fibromyalgia_The_Learning_ of_an_Illness_and_its_PNI_Correlates.

——, *The MindBody Code: How to Change the Beliefs that Limit Your Health, Longevity, and Success* (Boulder, CO: Sounds True, 2014).

——, *The MindBody Self: How Longevity Is Culturally Learned and the Causes of Health Are Inherited* (Carlsbad, CA: Hay House, Inc., 2017).

Maté, Gabor, *When the Body Says No: Understanding the Stress-Disease Connection* (Hoboken, NJ: John Wiley & Sons, 2011).

McClelland, David C. and Carol Kirshnit, "The Effect of Motivational Arousal through Films on Salivary Immunoglobulin A," *Psychology & Health* 2 (1988): dx.doi.org/10.1080/08870448808400343.

Miller, Gregory E., Edith Chen, and Karen J. Parker, "Psychological Stress in Childhood and Susceptibility to the Chronic Diseases of Aging: Moving toward a Model of Behavioral and Biological Mechanisms," *Psychological Bulletin* 137, no. 6 (Nov 2011): 959–997: dx.doi.org/10.1037/a0024768.

Orloff, Judith, *The Empath's Survival Guide: Life Strategies for Sensitive People* (Boulder, CO: Sounds True, 2017).

"Researchers Predict Cognitive Dissonance by Looking at Brain Activity," *Neuroscience News* (May 17, 2017): neurosciencenews.com/cognitive-dissonance-brain-activity-6709.

Richo, David, *How to Be an Adult in Relationships: The Five Keys to Mindful Loving* (Boston, MA: Shambhala Publications, Inc., 2002).

Roberts, Andrea L. et al, "Association of Trauma and Posttraumatic Stress Disorder with Incident Systemic Lupus Erythematosus (SLE) in a Longitudenal Cohort of Women," *Arthritis & Rheumatology,* Accepted Author Manuscript: doi:10.1002/art.40222.

Schoenthalter, Stephen J., "The Effect of Sugar on the Treatment and Control of Antisocial Behavior: A Double-Blind Study of an Incarcerated Juvenile Population," *International Journal of Biosocial Research* 3, no. 1 (1982): 1–9.

Schulze, L. et al, "Gray Matter Abnormalities in Patients with Narcissistic Personality Disorder," *Journal of Psychiatric Research* 47, no. 10 (October 2013): 1363–9.

Simon, George, *Character Disturbance: The Phenomenon of Our Age* (Marion, MI: Parkhurst Brothers Publishers, Inc., 2011).

———, "How to Recognize True (and False) Contrition," *A Cry for Justice* (March 4, 2013): cryingoutforjustice.com/2013/03/04/how-to-recognize-true-and-false-contrition-by-dr-george-simon-jr.

———, *In Sheep's Clothing: Understanding and Dealing with Manipulative People* (Marion, MI: Parkhurst Brothers Publishers, Inc., 2010).

Stojanovich, L. and D. Marisavljevich, "Stress as a Trigger of Autoimmune Disease," *Autoimmunity Reviews* 7, no. 3 (January 2008): 209–13.

Stout, Martha, *The Sociopath Next Door* (New York: Broadway Books, 2006).

Wolynn, Mark, *It Didn't Start with You: How Inherited Family Trauma Shapes Who We Are and How to End the Cycle* (New York: Penguin Books, 2017).

Van Veen, Vincent et al, "Neural Activity Predicts Attitude Change in Cognitive Dissonance," *Nature Neuroscience* 12 (2009): 1469–74: doi.org/10.1038/nn.2413.

Vernikos, Joan, *Sitting Kills, Moving Heals: How Everyday Movement Will Prevent Pain, Illness, and Early Death—and Exercise Alone Won't* (Fresno, CA: Quill Driver Books, 2011).

Villoldo, Alberto, *One Spirit Medicine: Ancient Ways to Ultimate Wellness* (Carlsbad, CA: Hay House, Inc., 2016).

INDEX

I

imagination, 164–66

immune system, 46, 53, 58–60, 123, 168

    autoimmune disorders, 45–47, 50–51, 58, 59

    IgA and, 143

    morals of, 55, 147

imprint removal process, 113–17

in-between, 103–4

inflammation, 46–48, 52–53, 57–59, 164, 168, 170, 172, 174, 184

inner child, 29–30, 104, 123–27

In Sheep's Clothing (Simon), 74, 83, 110

Institute for Relational Harm Reduction, 13

insulin, 48, 174, 180

intention, 164

iodine, 180–81

It Didn't Start with You: How Inherited Family Trauma Shapes Who We Are and How to End the Cycle (Wolynn), 25–26

It's a Man's World and a Woman's Universe (Allen), 148

J

Jerry Maguire, 29

Jesus, 28, 192

Journal of Psychiatric Research, 71

joy, 144–45, 147, 156, 193

    empathic, 147

Jung, Carl, 136

K

Kahn, Matt, 119, 120, 122–23, 141, 145

Kenney, Alexi, 198

Kent, Tami Lynn, 121

Kirshnit, Carol, 143

L

leaders, 198

LeShan, Lawrence, 59

Levine, Stephen, 133

Levy, Becca, 54

libido, 48

light, 132, 137. *See also* standing as the light

lightbulbs, 10

Lipton, Bruce, 54, 60

liver detox cycle, 177

loneliness, 104, 123, 124

longevity, 54–55, 197

love, 101, 113, 121–23, 160, 186

    Divine Love, 159–64, 173, 177, 193, 197

    self-love, 119–22, 130, 186

loving-kindness, 54–56, 147, 187

loyalty, 131, 133

Ludwig, David, 174

lupus, 50

M

macrophages, 58

magnesium, 176, 181

Magnesium Miracle, The (Dean), 181

malignant intuition, 30–31

Manhattan, 156

manipulation:

    tactics of, 79–80, 81, 84

    vulnerability to, 85–88

Martinez, Mario, 19, 52–56, 79, 94, 101, 128, 130, 140

Y

ACKNOWLEDGMENTS

First off, I truly have to thank all the energy vampires who are no longer in my life. Without you, I never would have learned what I have learned or have become the person I am today.

Huge gratitude to Reid Tracy, the president of Hay House, for being a champion for this book and especially the title. I so appreciate you having my back on this material, which, at first glance, appears to be a big U-turn for me. Except that it really isn't.

Margarete Nielsen, COO of Hay House, for her extraordinary ability to keep the ship of this entire publishing house afloat.

Laura Gray—my unflappable editorial genius who was with me every step of the way—from Maine to South Dakota and back again.

Anne Barthel—my Hay House editor extraordinaire whose skill and insight have made this project a real pleasure. And also made it a much better book.

Patricia Gift, vice president and acquisitions editor at Hay House—a true soul sister who just gets it on every level.

Richelle Fredson—head of publicity at Hay House—truly the most hilarious and effective publicist I have ever had the pleasure of working with.

The entire team at Hay House Radio. I just love my weekly Hay House radio show, *Flourish!*, and the global community of people I get to interact with regularly.

The whole staff at Hay House. I pinch myself that I get to work with such a simpatico, skilled, and great group.

Dr. George Simon and Sandra L. Brown, M.A.—huge gratitude for being pioneers in the field of character disorder, especially when it wasn't recognized by society in general and the mental health field in particular. Your courage and outstanding research have contributed enormously to this book and to the world at large.

Robert Palumbo, Ph.D.—thank you for the wisdom gleaned from 35 years as a skilled clinical psychologist who has taught me a great deal about character disorders and Cluster B individuals.

Hope Matthews, for all the years of assisting me in getting my story out of my fascia and retraining me for pain-free and joyful living.

Julie Hofheimer, whose ability to read unseen messages while doing massage is unparalleled.

Melanie Ericksen, Magical Mermaid Medicine Woman, for witnessing me through so many years of healing and growth and being an incredibly skilled and compassionate healer. Not to mention loyal friend.

Mike Perry—aka Thor—for demonstrating to me how fun, irreverent, helpful, knowledgeable, deep, Scorpionic, and reliable a man can be.

Paulina Carr—for all the loyal hours of service and troubleshooting over at the schoolhouse. And for your ability to take all of it in stride with a smile and laugh when the going gets a little crazy.

Janet Lambert—for keeping my financial house in order for years. As well as being a kick-ass ageless goddess role model with water skiing, sky diving, and scuba.

Coulson Duerksen, my online editor for drnorthrup. com. Thank you for being a tuned-in writer and editor who has your finger on the pulse of everything that is healthy and sustainable.

Pat McCabe—my household manager. For your magical presence, your practical skills, and your loyalty. I so appreciate you.

And finally, to Diane Grover—my CEO of everything, loyal samurai, keeper of the archives, witness to all the vampires, co-conspirator in enjoying bawdy humor, and wonderful, steady friend for all these years.

ABOUT THE AUTHOR

Christiane Northrup, M.D., board-certified ob/gyn, former assistant clinical professor of ob/gyn at the University of Vermont College of Medicine, *New York Times* best-selling author, is a visionary pioneer in women's health. After decades on the front lines of her profession as a practicing physician in obstetrics and gynecology, she is now dedicating her life to helping women truly flourish by learning how to enhance all that can go right with their bodies. Dr. Northrup is a leading proponent of medicine that acknowledges the unity of mind, body, emotions, and spirit. Internationally known for her empowering approach to women's health and wellness, she teaches women how to thrive at every stage of life and encourages them to create health on all levels by tuning in to their inner wisdom.

As a business owner, physician, former surgeon, mother, writer, and speaker, Dr. Northrup acknowledges our individual and collective capacity for growth, freedom, joy, and balance. She is also thrilled with her company, AmataLife, whose name is derived from Thai words meaning "ageless" and "eternal." This company is devoted to creating and distributing products to support women's health and beauty worldwide.

When she's not traveling, Dr. Northrup loves devoting her leisure time to dancing Argentine tango, going to the movies, getting together with friends and family, boating, playing the harp, and reading.

Dr. Northrup stays in touch with her worldwide community through her Internet radio show *Flourish!*, Facebook, Twitter, her monthly e-letter, and her website, drnorthrup.com.

Hay House Titles of Related Interest

YOU CAN HEAL YOUR LIFE, the movie,
starring Louise Hay & Friends
(available as a 1-DVD program, an expanded
2-DVD set, and an online streaming video)
Learn more at www.hayhouse.com/louise-movie

THE SHIFT, the movie,
starring Dr. Wayne W. Dyer
(available as a 1-DVD program, an expanded
2-DVD set, and an online streaming video)
Learn more at www.hayhouse.com/the-shift-movie

*BECOMING SUPERNATURAL: How Common People Are Doing
the Uncommon,* by Dr. Joe Dispenza

*HUMAN BY DESIGN: From Evolution by Chance to
Transformation by Choice,* by Gregg Braden

*THE MINDBODY SELF: How Longevity Is Culturally Learned and
the Causes of Health Are Inherited,* by Dr. Mario Martinez

*QUANTUM LOVE: Use Your Body's Atomic Energy to Create the
Relationship You Desire,* by Laura Berman, Ph.D.

*THE TAPPING SOLUTION FOR MANIFESTING YOUR GREATEST
SELF: 21 Days to Releasing Self-Doubt, Cultivating Inner Peace,
and Creating a Life You Love,* by Nick Ortner

All of the above are available at your local bookstore,
or may be ordered by contacting Hay House (see next page).

We hope you enjoyed this Hay House book. If you'd like to receive our online catalog featuring additional information on Hay House books and products, or if you'd like to find out more about the Hay Foundation, please contact:

Hay House, Inc., P.O. Box 5100, Carlsbad, CA 92018-5100
(760) 431-7695 or (800) 654-5126
(760) 431-6948 (fax) or (800) 650-5115 (fax)
www.hayhouse.com® • www.hayfoundation.org

———

Published and distributed in Australia by:
Hay House Australia Pty. Ltd., 18/36 Ralph St., Alexandria NSW 2015
Phone: 612-9669-4299 • *Fax:* 612-9669-4144 • www.hayhouse.com.au

Published and distributed in the United Kingdom by:
Hay House UK, Ltd., Astley House, 33 Notting Hill Gate, London W11 3JQ
Phone: 44-20-3675-2450 • *Fax:* 44-20-3675-2451 • www.hayhouse.co.uk

Published in India by: Hay House Publishers India,
Muskaan Complex, Plot No. 3, B-2, Vasant Kunj, New Delhi 110 070
Phone: 91-11-4176-1620 • *Fax:* 91-11-4176-1630 • www.hayhouse.co.in

Distributed in Canada by:
Raincoast Books, 2440 Viking Way, Richmond, B.C. V6V 1N2
Phone: 1-800-663-5714 • *Fax:* 1-800-565-3770 • www.raincoast.com

———

Access New Knowledge.
Anytime. Anywhere.

Learn and evolve at your own pace
with the world's leading experts.

www.hayhouseU.com